Salty

Praise for *Salty*

"These are the stories Lonnie would tell on dark nights in the wheel-house that would keep us in stitches. Prepare to be highly entertained!"
– Captain Eric Treece ("E.T.")
  S.S. *Wilfred Sykes* (Present)
  S.S. *Edward L. Ryerson* (2006-2009)

"Long ago, I had the pleasure of being a shipmate of Captain Lon Calloway aboard the S.S. *Sewell Avery* of the U.S. Steel Great Lakes Fleet, during the 1975 season, from fit-out in late March through to lay-up in November. When you would be stuck with people for what seemed an indefinite period, it was always good to know who your real pals could be. From the beginning to its seasonal end, Lon was my friend.

Together, we learned how to tie a draggin' bowline, and that, no, you can't actually go to the engine room to ask to borrow the bulkhead remover. We frequented Horseface Mary's in South Chicago and other notable sailor's taverns in Lorain and Conneaut, Ohio. We also learned to appreciate the astounding grandeur of the cobalt blue waters of eastern Lake Superior, and watched crystal-clear night skies from the boat deck.

I will never forget the howling pleasure of watching Lon entertain the tourists (and all his shipmates) at the Soo Locks, performing his perfected deck-ape routines handling heaving lines and cables after being lowered to the dock in the bos'n chair.

The stories of this man's long and fascinating maritime career found within these pages will entertain the hell out of you. I encourage you to cast off and begin the pleasurable journey to where this book will take you.

Congratulations Lon, your 'running lights are burning bright.' Happy reading to everyone."
– Peter K. Jongewaard
  Able Seaman, S.S. *Sewell Avery*
  US Steel Great Lakes Fleet, 1975

"Chapter after chapter, I found myself hanging on every word. Batten down the hatches and settle in for a wild, highly entertaining ride!"
 – Roger LeLievre
  Author/Editor of *Know Your Ships: Guide to Boats & Boatwatching on the Great Lakes & St. Lawrence Seaway*

"Working with Lon has always been an adventure. The weirdest situations arise and strangest people always seem to appear in his everyday life. If these tales don't surprise and entertain you then you might want to reflect a little because you may have been one of his encounters."
 – Captain Garth J. Law ("Sharkey")
  Arnold Mackinac Island Ferry Line

"I have known Lonnie Calloway for over 15 years and sailed on a number of vessels with him. Lonnie is a straight shooter and someone of strong moral fiber, he is a great shipmate and an all-around good guy with an awesome sense of humor. He has done many things in his merchant marine career, some of which he will share with you in the following pages. I hope you enjoy these stories as much as I do.
Semper Paratus and God Speed, Lonnie."
 – Joe Parsons II
  Chief Engineer, Steam, Motor and Gas Turbine,
   Unlimited Horsepower
  United States Merchant Marine

"As a former Coastie, I served with Lon aboard the U.S. Coast Guard cutter *Woodrush* (WLB-407) in Sitka, Alaska. We worked hard and partied harder. It was a blast!

This is an epic read. I could smell the salt air, and feel the spray and the deck rolling under my feet!"

– William Zimmerman
FDNY-Fire Dept. of New York
32-Year Veteran: Engine 222 ("Triple Deuce")

"For over 40 years, it's been my pleasure to have called Captain Calloway my watch partner, shipmate, and once, my best man. Traditionally, sea stories begin one of two ways: 'It was a dark and stormy night,' or 'Now this is no shit.' Since I was with Lon on many of his adventures and can vouch for the accuracy of the insanities, the second beginning would be appropriate. Enjoy the book!"

– Rick ("Ricardo") Gay
Able Seaman (AB) Unlimited
U.S. Merchant Marine

"For those of you in search of the true tales of a modern-day Ernest Hemingway, the sea stories in this book will not disappoint! Captain Lonnie delivers true shipboard experiences of his life on the seas told in an uninhibited and humorous manor. This book chronicles tales of a fading era through the lives of 'true men of the sea'."

– Captain William R. LaParl
Unlimited Master/First Class Pilot–Great Lakes

Salty

The Colorful Adventures of
a Well-Seasoned Seadog

Lon Calloway

Published by Phoenesse LLC

ISBN: 9781732735859

The stories in this book are the author's personal recollections of real-life events. Names have been changed to protect the privacy of the many shipmates mentioned.

On the cover: Lon Calloway on the stern of the tug *Zephyr*, towing the freight barge *Mercury* and taking seriously heavy rolls in the Gulf of Alaska. Photo taken by shipmate Richard Gay. Cover inset photo courtesy of Tim Calloway.

For Lisa,
my favorite Boatnerd and steady companion.
Without your loving support and encouragement,
these stories would not be on paper.

Contents

Introduction

For me, it was always about the motion. Not just the gentle rocking of a ship that made sleep such a pleasure, nor the heart-pumping thrill of going weightless in my rack as we tossed our way across some deep body of water. It was the fact I was on the move. *That's* always been the best part. Going to sleep in one place and waking up in another was like being on a magic carpet.

It's true, I dodged some shit with this way of life. Or as one early girlfriend put it, "Getting back on that boat is pretty damn convenient for you, isn't it?" I admit, I wasn't always there for those who stayed behind. But this has been my life, and over the decades I have become better and better at living it.

Through all the ups and downs, I've managed to live the most colorful life I could have imagined for myself, and I'm delighted to share some of the highlights with you. I hope you'll be OK with the language. Truth be told, cursing is what made the ships go. So here it is: shipboard authentic and salty as hell. I could not tell these tales any other way.

– Captain Lon Calloway

1

Close Encounters of the "Turd" Kind

Alaska has always been a magnet for tourists and adventure seekers. Especially the beautiful snowcapped mountains, deep blue fjords and protected waterways of Southeast Alaska's Alexander archipelago. At the top of the 900-mile Inside Passage—a watery network of passes and straits stretching 900 miles from Bellingham, Washington to Skagway, Alaska—the scenic waterfalls and glaciers attract thousands of visitors each year.

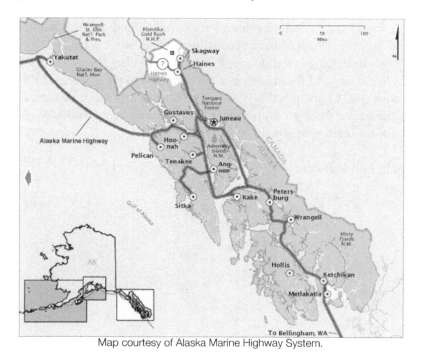

Map courtesy of Alaska Marine Highway System.

Map of the marine highway known as Inside Passage.

While long a destination for hardy travelers, the 1980s brought a boom in cruise ship visitors. Cruise ships began calling frequently at the Southeast Alaskan ports of Ketchikan, Juneau, Skagway and Sitka on their way to and from Glacier Bay National Park.

What began with older style cruise ships like the *Pacific Princess* of *Love Boat* fame quickly grew to be replaced by floating monsters regularly disgorging thousands of passengers at a time on sleepy Alaskan villages. The ships would travel by night, dropping anchor in a new harbor before dawn. Daybreak found masses of passengers hitting the town. Then back on the ship and up anchor by noon and on to the next stop.

Realizing the potential goldmine being delivered to their front doors, local entrepreneurs began creating mini adventures to sell as "shore excursions" to the disembarking tourists. Tours had to be safe, above all, and fairly brief. The ships ran on a tight schedule and absolutely needed to depart on time. Towns scrambled to tap into the new cash opportunities.

A company called Alaska Travel Adventures, or ATA, was formed by a group of businessmen. They set out to create Alaskan experiences in the cities of Juneau, Ketchikan and Sitka. They had to be classy outings to appeal to the high standards of the cruise lines, as they would be selling the tours on board ahead of each port stop. They definitely succeeded there.

In Juneau, ATA offered whitewater rafting down the Mendenhall River, past icebergs and glaciers. In Ketchikan, the gig was the opportunity to paddle a Tlinghat war canoe across an inland lake and enjoy a salmon bake in a tent on the far shore. In Sitka, it was a guided tour in a 20-foot inflatable Zodiac around St. Lazaria Island, a national Marine Wildlife Preserve and home to thousands of seabirds including tufted puffins.

These tours weren't cheap, each costing in the neighborhood of $100 per person. Cruise ship passengers would buy the shore excursions on board the ships from a staff member called the "shore ex." The day before the ship's arrival in a given port, the shore ex would call ATA with a count of how many excursions had been sold. This allowed ATA to staff the tour appropriately.

The best trip was the Marine Wildlife Tour in Sitka visiting the seabird rookeries on St. Lazaria Island. According to Wikipedia:

> St. Lazaria Island is a nesting bird colony located 20 miles out to sea on the outer edge of Sitka Sound. It was dedicated as a National Wildlife Preserve in 1909 by Theodore Roosevelt and received official wilderness designation from congress in 1970. It was added to the Alaska Maritime National Wildlife Refuge in 1980.
>
> St. Lazaria Island is a very rugged looking island. Its direct exposure to the Pacific Ocean makes it an ideal bird habitat. The Island is a volcanic plug, a remnant of an old and eroded volcano, a cousin to the nearby extinct volcano Mt. Edgecumbe on Kruzof Island. There are many cliffs that can reach 90 feet high and shoot straight down into

the ocean as well as sea level caves that can be explored on a calm day.

Just about all the wildlife on St. Lazaria is birds. On the island there are:

- 250,000 breeding pairs of Fork-tailed storm petrals and Leach's storm petrals
- 4-5000 common and thick billed Murres
- 1,500-2000 breeding pairs of Tufted Puffins
- 1000 breeding pairs of Rhinoceros auklets

Other less populous species include pigeon guillemots, glaucous winged gulls, ancient murrelets, Cassin's auklets, bald eagles, peregrine falcons and black oystercatchers. In nesting areas on the island the bird density can reach 7000 birds per acre."

Wikipedia contributors, "Saint Lazaria Wilderness," *Wikipedia, The Free Encyclopedia*, (accessed March 25, 2020).

The main problem with St. Lazaria was its isolation and location 20 miles out in the ocean, as the tour had to be back within the four-hour time limit or miss the ship. ATA solved this issue by building a fast, 149-passenger catamaran—also called a "cat"—they named the *Golden Spirit*, in an attempt to capture some of the glamour and romance of Alaska's gold rush days. It was an unfortunate name choice though, as jaded locals immediately dubbed her the "Golden Shower," much to the company's disgust.

Patrick, one of the tour guides, zooms past
the *Golden Spirit* in a fast-moving Zodiac.

The concept was to pick up the passengers from the cruise ship with the cat, and ferry them in comfort to St. Lazaria. They would serve the tourists coffee, tea and fresh cinnamon rolls on the way out, and a potent concoction of Irish whiskey, coffee and Baileys—called "Baranof Bombers"—on the way back.

The passengers would be met at the island by 20-foot long 15-passenger inflatable Zodiacs operated by a captain/guide. The Zodiacs would pull up to the stern of the cat and pick up their load of clients and depart on a slow cruise around the island, giving a nature talk along the way and observing as many varieties of birds as possible.

When the tour was first being organized, it came to the company's attention that the Zodiac captains would need to be licensed by the Coast Guard. I saw a "help wanted" ad in the Sitka's Daily Sentinel looking for people interested in running Zodiac tours. I thought it might be interesting so I went to the meeting. I was surprised to find a Coast Guard officer present who immediately began handing out tests.

This was unexpected. I thought this was just an informative session. *Oh well…let's see what we got here.* After four years as a navigation rate in the Coast Guard, this test was ridiculously easy. I burned through it and wasn't surprised I passed, but was shocked by what came next.

The owner of ATA had some political pull in Juneau and it was in the state's best interest to make this shore excursion business happen. A basic six-passenger license —or "6-pack"—would not do, as each Zodiac would be carrying 15 people. The next bump up was a 100-ton license, which was way overkill for an inflatable boat. As a result, the Coast Guard was prevailed upon to come up with an "in-between" license specific to this tour. They invented a license that read: "Master of small inflatable passenger vessels under five gross tons, while engaged in the Sitka Marine Wildlife Tour, within a mile of the mothership, and the mothership is underway."

This was unbelievable. An inflatable boat with five-gross-ton displacement would be massive! The license was issued on official U.S. Coast Guard Merchant Marine Officer stock with an actual Merchant Marine Officer issue number at the top. This was the real deal, but restricted to this particular tour. I've never seen anything like it before or since.

That issue number counted and remained the starting point the Coast Guard used when tracking my license progress for my entire career. Every license I received after that was considered an "upgrade" and required fewer exams as a result. It was really crazy! They obviously never thought it through, because we guys in the first batch of Zodiac captains they hired were the only ones who got that politically motivated "special circumstance" license.

A boatload of tourists leaving the *Golden Spirit*.

After many years climbing the maritime ladder and receiving my unlimited tonnage master's license, this first one is still my favorite. In five seasons, I made thousands of dollars with that goofy license, just part-timing. The job was interesting and the management was top-notch. It was probably the most fun I ever had at work!

The best part was playing with the boats: 20-foot Zodiacs with at least 40-horse outboards. The boat I used had a 90-horse Evinrude. I called her "Black Lightning" and she was a rocket.

Ninety horses drove that airbag along like a guided missile. I moved the 30-gallon fuel tank all the way forward and lashed it down to balance the weight of the motor. We had to run out to St. Lazaria empty to meet the cat with the clients and it was always a rush screaming through the waves 20 miles straight out to sea. There would usually be 3-5 boats running out together and we had a blast chasing each other and just generally screwing around. There were times when the cat went back to town for another load and left us out there for several hours free to drive around and explore.

One of the coolest experiences I ever had in Alaska happened during one of those layovers. I was by myself cruising along the beach when I spotted a large humpback whale heading into a little cove. The entrance was narrow and the cove wasn't that long so I suspected he would be coming back out soon. I got right in the middle of the entrance, shut the motor off, and lifted the prop. I was just quietly floating there waiting.

Soon I saw ripples approaching, then as they got closer I saw the long gray length of the humpback break the surface. As he moved majestically along, unhurried, I could see algae and barnacles clinging to his dark skin. He must have been 30 feet long and as he got closer, he kind of rolled a little on his side. As he approached, I was looking right into a huge eye just cracking the surface. In awe, I stared at him while he stared back at me.

Just another day at the office.

Passing under me, my boat was lifted up as it slid easily down the whale's back. He cleared the entrance and I looked back to see his giant fluke lift, dripping into the air as he gracefully disappeared into the depths. I was frozen with delight and didn't move for several minutes, my heart thudding in my chest. I had considered trying for a picture but I'm glad I didn't. The moment is best preserved in my mind.

Different cruise lines catered to a varied clientele and our passengers covered a wide cross section of the world's population. We had many Japanese tourists and often they didn't speak English. Their tour company provided interpreters, usually young college-age women, to accompany each boat and translate our information. As we circled St. Lazaria and gave our spiel, she would translate questions from her group. It was always fun listening to them try to put the names of the birds and other Alaskan terms into Japanese.

I pointed out a tug and barge passing by inbound to Sitka. She looked puzzled as I explained what a tugboat was and what it did. She began to translate but stopped and seemed to search for a word. Finally she brightened and I heard her say, "Tugboato." *Ah.*

Her people all nodded, smiled and repeated: "Tugboato."

There was a cave on the island that was a nesting area for pelagic cormorants. There were hundreds of them. The cave was large enough that we could drive our boats inside, turn around and slowly putt back out. Folks really liked it.

Usually the first thing we would do while waiting for the cat was to drive quickly by the cave. This caused the birds to fly out in a flock, dumping their loads in a veritable storm of bird poop. We were trying to at least limit the amount of guano there might be flying through the air later. We called that "shittin' and gittin'."

A raft cruising the beach of St. Lazaria Island near the dark cave (toward the right) we drove inside.

When we had passengers in the rafts, they were sometimes given rain ponchos to wear over their clothes to protect them from aerial assaults of this nature. With over half a million birds wheeling through the air, we called parts of the tour: *Close Encounters of the "Turd" Kind*. I know, it's bad…but still funny.

We had a diver that went out with us, anchored a boat near the island and went diving for samples of undersea specimens. He brought up sea urchins, sea cucumbers, different species of starfish, crabs and whatever else he could find. As we circled the island we took turns pulling alongside and letting our guests see and sometimes hold these fascinating creatures.

One trip I had a mixed load of American tourists from one ship and Japanese tourists from another. We pulled up to the floating petting zoo and started showing off the residents. Handing over a spiny sea urchin, the Americans gingerly held it, ooh'd and ahh'd and passed it along. It got to the Japanese contingent and the first man to hold it flipped it over and rammed his fingers through the shell, bringing out a dripping handful of gooey sea urchin guts and gobbling it down. Grinning and nodding his head, he passed it around with all his party taking a scoop, then tossed the now-empty shell over the side.

The Americans were frozen in shock and a little girl started to cry. They all turned to see what I had to say. I had nothing. "Now if you look to your right you can see a bald eagle soaring over that treetop," I said, dropping the line on the zoo and motoring the hell out of there, the empty urchin shell bobbing pitifully in my wake.

A couple days later I get a call from Jay, our site boss in Sitka. I guess the Americans complained to the shore ex who passed it up the line. "What the hell's going on over there?" Jay sputtered. "I heard from the Feds at the National Park Service that my tour was allowing passengers to kill and eat the inhabitants of a National Wildlife Preserve."

"Jesus, Jay, if you fed them better on the way out this might not happen. It was a Japanese tour and they wanted sushi. Nothin' I could do about it," I said.

"Well, next time warn them ahead of time this ain't a picnic."

"Will do, Boss. Will do."

When it was too rough to make the trip out to St. Lazaria, we had a fallback tour spot called the Siganaka Island group. Close in to town and well protected, it was a group of uninhabited islands in a cluster with narrow winding waterways separating them. There was a lot of wildlife out there: seals, sea otters, eagles, Sitka black-tailed deer, and even occasionally whales.

It wasn't a zoo though and seeing any or all those critters on any given day was not guaranteed. More than a few of our clients didn't understand that. They paid their $100, dammit, and had a checklist for what they expected to see. We did all we could to provide an interesting tour, locating an eagle nest ahead of time and even bringing out a few fish to salt the beach and get the eagles and otters in close.

We learned about part of our tour being "show biz," and the importance of making our clients feel they got their money's worth. No matter the weather, we were taught to tell our passengers: "You folks are lucky to be here today." If it was sunny: "You're lucky to have such a nice day." If it was raining: "You're lucky to have the opportunity to experience this beautiful rain forest in its natural state." *Lucky, lucky, lucky!*

Morning fog on the way to meet the ship.

The regular raft guides understood this and did a great job of giving folks a good tour. One time however, we were shorthanded and needed another guide to fill in. Since they had to have a license, our choices were extremely limited. I called an old tugboat buddy of mine to see if he was interested. Johnny was a crabby old goat but a nice guy. Pretty crusty with no filter, but I thought he might come across as "Alaska Authentic."

We gave Johnny a boatload of tourists and sent him off. As the tours were returning I could tell there was a little discontent in Johnny's boat. One lady seemed to be really giving him hell and I could see Johnny shaking his head and talking back. *Oh shit.*

I got to the boat before anybody else and helped the lady off. She was sputtering mad. "That man is the rudest person I've ever met," she stormed, pointing at Johnny. I look at him and he gives me a shrug. I calm her down, assure her that I'm the boss (I wasn't), and that I will definitely fire that rude bastard. I didn't know what he did but had no doubt that it was something.

I schmooze the old girl up, flirting my ass off and leaving her smiling. Dodged that bullet. I didn't want another call from Jay, and hiring Johnny was my idea.

We got the boats back and grabbed a stool at the Pioneer Bar for our usual post tour roundup. "So Johnny," I say, "What the hell did you do to Granny?"

"Aw, Jesus, Lonnie, she wouldn't shut up. 'When do we see the bear, when do we see the bear,'… on and on till my ears bled. I told her, 'This ain't a zoo,' but that didn't stop her. It was still 'Bear Bear Bear, Bitch Bitch Bitch'…reminded me of me last three ex-wives. I had enuf and told her 'Listen Lady, jist shut ur hole…you have as much chance of seeing a bear today as you have of seeing Santa Claus.' So fuck this tourist shit. I'm jist gonna go back to towin' logs."

"Sure thing, Johnny, thanks for the help."

But he was right about the bear.

See ya in town at the Pioneer Bar!

2
One Flew *Out* of the Cuckoo's Nest

When you work on a boat, who you get for shipmates is the luck of the draw. Sometimes lifelong friendships develop, but many times you discover you're trapped on a steel island with guys that should be in a mental asylum. As the months pass they never get better, only get worse. Occasionally, the other crew members warn you: "Watch out for Billy, he's crazy as a shithouse rat." As an officer, I always appreciated the heads-up. More often though, I had to discover who the loonies were myself.

There's no escape. The wackos are on board with you 24/7, watching, plotting, waiting for a chance to get even for some imagined slight. It's not paranoia. A few years back, a chief engineer with a Great Lakes company was asleep in his room when a disgruntled crewman snuck in and stabbed him dozens of times with a screwdriver. Luckily it was a Philips-head screwdriver, and since they were only puncture wounds, that saved his life. Lesson here is if you plan to kill your boss with a screwdriver, use a slot-head and wiggle it around.

For years I never bothered to lock my door, but after hearing that I made sure it was firmly bolted before I closed my eyes. I also went out of my way to befriend the psychos, chatting them up, asking about their hobbies—besides murder and mayhem—and feigning a deep interest in Star Wars trivia and UFOs. My hope was that when the slaughter started, the wack job du jour would pass by my door like the Angel of Death, with the voice in his head chanting "Lon's good...no kill...must kill *captain*," and me trying to put my voice in his head, "Yes, Lon's your friend...you like Lon...must kill *bad* captain." Hey, self-preservation.

Winter of 2003, I'm second mate on the M/V (Motor Vessel) *Buffalo*, a 630-foot iron ore freighter operated by the American Steamship Company, or ASC. It was good-naturedly referred to on the Lakes as "Arab Steamship Company" due to the large number of resident aliens from Dearborn's Yemenite community carried as crew.

On the *Buffalo*, our "resident crazy" was a young deckhand named Stevie. Stevie was full-blown nuts, but a good worker. Because he more than pulled his weight on deck, the crew overlooked the tinfoil lining in his helmet and his constant efforts to convince whoever he could corner that aliens walk among us. I always thought, "Yes they do Stevie, and I'm talking to one right now." I considered him fairly harmless, but never turned my back on him in case he had a slot-head screwdriver in his pocket.

The *Buffalo* loaded limestone regularly in either the ports of Calcite (Rogers City, Michigan) or Stoneport (Alpena, Michigan). We got our groceries from a ship chandler out of R.C. The crew used that address for mail as it was quicker to receive if the grocery guy brought it out than to wait for the mail boat in Detroit, or the marine post office at the Soo Locks, up on the Canadian border in Sault Ste Marie, Michigan

It was late December when the *Buffalo* switched runs from the stone trade to what was called the "ore train," a line of ships steadily hauling taconite from Silver Bay Minnesota to Lake Erie ports for winter stockpile. Stevie had ordered some long johns and winter gloves to be delivered through the mail to the grocery guy. Before he received them we switched runs and didn't go to the stone ports anymore that season. Stevie was getting wound up. *He wanted his stuff!*

The captain, Don, was a good guy and tried to help by calling and getting Stevie's order sent on to meet us, either at the Soo or Silver Bay. Unfortunately, late in the season, with all the delays, last minute changed orders and general confusion, his packages just kept missing us. Stevie was livid. *It had to be a conspiracy!*

He was certain the Arabs on board were responsible, particularly a young Yemeni guy named Mohammed, who the crew called "Mo." Mo was a nice kid, eager to please, just delighted to be on a ship and making good money. He had recently become a father and proudly carried photos of his family in his pocket wherever he went. Mo didn't have anything to do with Stevie's missing long underwear. Stevie was convinced otherwise.

As port after port vanished in our wake with no package for Stevie, he really started to come undone. He complained constantly, and accused everybody. At meals, he stared and glowered at Mo. Finally the chief engineer told him to "just shut the fuck up." The first assistant engineer jumped in and called him a "stupid bastard" and made fun of his tinfoil hat. *Uh-oh*, I thought. *You guys need to be careful here. Stevie's fuse is lit.*

Talking to Stevie after lunch I told him to ignore those guys. He looked at me slyly and said, "Oh, they're on the list." *Better them than me,* I thought. I reported it to Don and he shrugged it off. "Season's almost over, everybody's a little bats."

Meanwhile, I found out that Stevie was having a lot of phone contact with his mother, who I suspected may be where he got his world view, raging that the Arabs were stealing his mail and that the captain was in on it. I did my best to talk him down a bit, but pretty sure I wasn't making much headway. I did tell the chief and the first that they were numbers one and two on Stevie's "hit" parade, and might want to keep their doors locked.

Next to the last trip of the season, destination: Fairport, Ohio. Stevie's constant accusations and rants are getting out of hand, but he's generally being ignored. We pull into Fairport, crunching through the ice, and see our dock *filled* with law enforcement vehicles. Ohio Staties, Fairport City police, sheriff, Coast Guard, FBI, and even a black SUV we found out belonged to Homeland Security.

Don calls down on the radio and says that after we tie up, all crew need to report to the mess deck (dining room). *Wow, this is weird. Never seen this before.* I got the ship spotted in position to start the unload and head in to see what's going on. The whole crowd of cops is aboard by this time, some clustered in the crews mess, some in the passageway, while others are setting up an inter-rogation room next door in the officer's dining room. You couldn't move for all the uniforms. Two large men in long black trench coats are standing by the door. I get a glimpse of a sling and the barrel of an Uzi machine gun. *Holy shit.*

The crew is seated around the tables dead quiet. I stick my head in the door and Uzi growls at me, "Grab a seat and no talking." Then he adds in the same tone of voice, "Eat a cookie."

They have Mo in the other room, just grilling him. I found out later it was about Stevie's mail. But Mo's crying because he thinks he's on his way back to Yemen. After they let Mo come back in, pale and trembling, they take Stevie. He's only on the hot seat for 10 minutes when the FBI guy sticks his head in the door and says to Uzi, "We found the shaky wheel on this bus." It didn't take long for them to get Stevie's number, especially since he was carrying his tinfoil-lined hard hat and babbling about aliens. Mo was off the hook.

The Federal goons, the Ohio Staties, the Fairport cops and the sheriff are gone in a blink, leaving us all stunned and wondering, *What just happened?* The Coast Guard figured since they were already there they might as well inspect our safety gear, much to Don's displeasure. Since he knew I was ex-Coast Guard, I was assigned to accompany the inspector. Or as Don put it, "You know how to talk to those assholes."

Turns out the inspector and I did have some common Coast Guard experi-ences and once we got talking he told me the rest of the story. Seems after Ste-vie repeatedly aired his suspicions on the phone to his Mom, she called the FBI. She reported that Arab nationals were stealing U.S. Mail on a U.S. Merchant Marine ship. Since this was barely two years after 9/11, that hit all the red but-tons: FBI for mail theft, Coast Guard for Merchant Marine vessel, Homeland Security for the Arab connection, and the Ohio Staties, city police and sheriff probably because it was a slow day in Fairport and they didn't want to miss out.

Since Stevie hadn't committed any crime except being crazy, they left him on the boat. I was shocked. Stevie was still ranting and raging, even more than usual. But again, being a good guy, Don didn't want to just kick him off in frozen midwinter Ohio. He decided to let him stay on the boat, at least up to the Soo. I thought that was a big mistake. Too much time to do crazy unpredictable damage.

Upbound in the Detroit River, I was in the front window piloting the boat. Don was relaxing in the captain's recliner. I asked him why Stevie was still on board. He told me he wasn't worried about it. I casually said, "Well, I wouldn't sweat it Cap, you know you're on his death list, but you're only number three. He lives down on A deck, same as the chief and the first, so he'll likely murder them right away. You probably don't have to worry. By the time he gets way up here to your room, his arms will be tired from swinging that ax." Don just looks at me and doesn't say a thing. There's quiet for 15 minutes. Next thing I hear is him on the telephone asking the Coast Guard in Detroit to come get Stevie. They did.

I still locked my door. What if Stevie was right about the aliens among us, and they all carried slot-head screwdrivers?

3

Southern Exposure

Commercial shipping on the Great Lakes is, by virtue of their northern latitudes, seasonal. Winter shuts down the inland water routes with an icy fist. Shivering crews pack their gear for a couple months by the home fires, and ships go into the yards for much-needed maintenance.

In November of 2001, returning from a 60-day relief job in Hawaii, I was reluctant to go from warm tropical breezes to the frigid blasts of Lake Superior. Things were slow on the Lakes, so I called a shipping agent I knew who placed crew around the country. Long story short, Wayne hooked me up with a job as first mate on a tug working out of Mobile, Alabama.

A Great Lakes tug company based in Cleveland had recently won a towing contract with an Alabama cement plant. Their tug, *Mohawk*, would be used to tow a bulk cement barge, the *Industrial #1*, from Theodore, Alabama—an industrial port on Mobile Bay—to a cement receiving facility in Tampa, Florida. It was straight across the Gulf of Mexico, a distance of roughly 400 miles as the crow flies.

The *Mohawk* was built in 1960. She was 91 feet long with a breadth of 29 feet, and her two 12-cylinder electric marine diesels put out 2400 horses. She was a gutsy little tug and had spent her career around the Great Lakes, towing small barges and assisting with fleeting work in Cleveland on the Cuyahoga River She was built in the canal style, meaning she was very long and low with a wheelhouse that could be raised and lowered hydraulically to get under low bridges in Cleveland. The company sent her down the Mississippi to a shipyard in New Orleans to be refitted for ocean towing. It was necessary to make several modifications to receive certification by the American Bureau of Ships.

I flew to New Orleans the day after Christmas, leaving Traverse City in a blizzard. I arrived to sunshine in the Big Easy and was met at the airport by the captain. Ralph was a middle-aged Cajun, right out of the bayou. Slightly overweight with red hair and a permanently flushed complexion, he was wearing sweat-stained khaki work clothes and had a big plug of Redman bulging his cheek. The first words out of his mouth were, "Har ya doin' cousin' call me Ralph you liketa fish?"

I really didn't do much fishing but thought I better respond with an enthusiastic, "Hell yeah!" I threw my bag in the back of a grimy shipyard pickup and we headed to the river, with Ralph talking nonstop to bring me up to speed with the "big pitcher," as he called it.

We got to the shipyard and, with the Mississippi River rolling by, I get my first look at my new home. I was not impressed. Blocked up out of the water, high and dry, she was a dismal sight. Festooned with power cords and compressed air hoses, the ear-splitting shriek of multiple grinders and clanging of hammers made talking impossible. Workmen swarmed over her like ants. She was filthy, with a thick coating of dirt, sandblast grit and paint chips covering every square inch of her half-stripped hull.

Ralph introduced me to Bob, the engineer, an Ohio hillbilly from the woods around Athens. Wearing a paint-spattered flannel shirt and glasses so dirty I didn't know how he could see, he stuck out a greasy paw to shake. "Welcome to the 'Hawk,'" was his shouted greeting. "Who'd you piss off up in Cleveland to get sent down here?" Looking around, I could see his point.

The next two weeks were spent working on the boat during the day, mainly scrubbing out my room, and kicking back in a nice hotel room every night. But the time quickly came to move onto the boat and it was with reluctance I turned in my hotel key.

We were finally crewed up with a captain, mate, two engineers and two deckhands who would be standing six hours on and six hours off, round the clock: one guy in the wheelhouse, one guy in the engine room, and a deckhand roaming around (or more often watching movies in the air-conditioned galley). No cook, so guys took turns. Only two Yankees and four southern boys, so it was red beans, rice and grits every day.

I had a decent single room with a porthole on the main deck of the tug, as did Ralph and Bob. When the rest of the crew arrived and took a look at the crew's quarters below deck, both original deckies quit on the spot. The rooms down below were dark, dank and moldy, with poor ventilation and wafting a nasty smell we could never identify.

This would prove to be an ongoing issue. Guys would quit after a single trip. Their replacements would show up, take one look, and toss their gear right back on the dock. They often caught the same cab that brought them down. This happened almost every trip when we first started running. I got to know the Seafarers International Union (deckhand union) dispatcher very well.

We ran through at least a dozen one-trip deckhands in the first couple months. We finally got two guys to stick. Jorge, a cocky little runt, was from Brazil and smart enough to know when he had a great-paying gig. The other one was a young guy from Guatemala named Bernardo. Bernardo was a refugee who had had a tough life. He spoke halting English.

When I took Bernardo down into the forepeak of the tug to show him his room, I expected him to quit like all the rest. Looking at the dark damp grubby room with the two bunks bolted to the wall, instead of storming off in disgust, he looked at me with a pleased expression. "All this for me?" he asked.

"Damn skippy, Bernardo. All yours." He couldn't believe his good fortune. (I thought, *Americans are entitled, whining pussies.*) He settled in as happy as a clam and I never heard a complaint out of him.

Truthfully, the whole program was shaky. Quarters sucked, the air conditioning was quirky, and the tug was totally unsuited for ocean travel. But you either work with what you have or you get off the boat. Ask Bernardo. I decided to stick around for a while.

The cement plant in Mobile Bay was in the industrial port of Theodore, a busy staging port for offshore oil rig support. A Wild West mentality prevailed. The bare-bones, cinder-block bars up the street were packed and rowdy with roughnecks, rig hands, boat crews and assorted flotsam from the oil rigs. Anything goes. The common decorative theme in every joint was leaning toward Confederate flags and posters of skeletons in shredded rebel gray running over piles of Yankee dead. It's not the "Civil War" down here, it's the "War of Northern Aggression," and they're still fighting it. *Yeeeeeehaw!*

Crew boats and supply boats churned back and forth to a city of offshore rigs around the clock. Huge container ships, tankers and tugboats towing ocean barges traveled in and out of the bay in a long line. The channel from Theodore out to the sea buoy was over 30 miles long but only 400 feet wide. Outside of the channel, water was too shallow to navigate. To complicate things even more, the tide changed twice a day. It was either ebbing (rushing out) or flooding (pouring in), with a brief period of calm (slack) in between.

**Jorge and Bernardo, with *Industrial #1*
looming in the background.**

As mentioned, the "Coon-asses" (locals) were still fighting the Civil War and quickly noticed my "Yankee accent" on the radio. I got derogatory comments and general abuse every time I made a security call. It didn't take me long to start drawling like I just crawled "outta da swump." On the Great Lakes, a meeting agreement between ships would be like, "Good Evening, Cap, I propose meeting on one whistle, port to port." Down on the Gulf, it was, "Hey 'dere Cuz...see ya onda one...OK?"

I started telling the locals that my daddy was born in Virginia (he was) and I was raised in Michigan against my will. Derision changed to sympathy. Me: "Yeah, screw them Blue-belly bastards and pass me them grits."

After finally leaving N'awlins in our wake, we got to Mobile and met up with our barge, the *Industrial #1*. This thing is massive. It's a self-unloading, floating warehouse that's 400 feet long, 75 feet wide and 40 feet deep. Towing this monstrosity, the *Mohawk* looked like a mouse trying to drag an elephant. The tug had nowhere near enough power to handle this beast. But we hook up and away we go.

Trying to control the *Industrial #1* with the little *Mohawk* was a nightmare. If we were traveling outbound on the ebb, the current wanted to push the barge right up our ass. Going out against a flood meant cranking the wheel like a madman trying to prevent the barge from running either out of the channel and grounding us, or into another ship and sinking us.

Mohawk leaving Theodore, lining out *Industrial #1*.

The only thing we could do was bring the barge right up tight behind the tug in a desperate attempt to maintain some control. It made the hair stand up on my neck to look back and see that huge shadow looming behind us. I was getting a stiff neck from constantly swiveling back to see where it was now. Finally Ralph told me, "Hey cuz, don't even bother eyeballin' that prick...it'll jist scare ya." Words of wisdom.

Industrial #1 sneakin' up behind me in Tampa Bay.

Three times during my nine months of "Southern exposure," the *Industrial #1* went aground in Mobile Bay. Every time, it was because Ralph didn't check the tide/current tables. I always calculated the times for Mobile Bay as it was easier to leave on falling flood, hit slack water at the mouth, and let the increasing ebb shoot us out to sea like a champagne cork. It made a huge difference in how the barge towed. Ralph didn't think it mattered.

In the "coon-ass navy," as all the rig tenders and crew boats were called, they left port on a schedule set by the oil companies. They had lots of power and no barge, so it really didn't matter much to them. Ralph couldn't wrap his brain around the fact that we "weren't huntin' the same possum" as those guys, and it really mattered a lot when we departed.

He would have us depart apparently on a whim, tides be damned. Then it was string the *Industrial #1* out behind us and start cranking the wheel, fighting either max flood or max ebb. We were wrestling the barge all over the fairway and in the process scaring the piss out of incoming pilots.

The barge would take off in a direction all her own, and when loaded her inertia would drag the *Mohawk* backwards along with her. When that happens, your asshole puckers up so tight you won't shit for a week. As the barge went out of the channel far enough, she would plow up on the sandy bottom and there we would sit, hard aground. If it was low tide, we could wait for high tide and with luck float off. If it was high tide, we would have to wait through a complete tide cycle and then get another tug to put a line on the barge and pull us off.

Once we were piled up so far out of the channel it took three tugs to pull us out. That's massively expensive, and it eventually cost Ralph his job. It's also professionally embarrassing to have it happen repeatedly and to be sitting there for all the other boats to comment on as they zoom past.

The channel into Theodore met the Mobile Bay channel at a 90-degree junction. The plant always sent an assist tug out to help us make that corner and get tied up. We would set up a rendezvous appointment whenever we got close coming in. One night I relieved Ralph at midnight approaching the Mobile Bay entrance buoy. We had a rendezvous with the assist tug for 6 a.m. but we were already past slack tide and approaching the flood. The tide would be behind us and pushing.

I told Ralph, "We better do donuts out here until she slacks again and starts to ebb, or we won't be able to control the barge."

"Naw, cuz…we be OK…it's a clear night, head 'er in," he mumbles around his chaw. *A clear night? That has nothing to do with anything,* I think to myself. *I bet he has a date in town.* So I get to agonize all night trying to slow down enough to make the junction at 0600 and keep the barge from killing us in the meantime. *Lucky me.*

Right away it's a struggle. I'm trying to drag my feet enough to meet our ETA, but the flood tide is pushing the barge faster than the tug's going. All I can do is winch it in as close behind me as I dare and start fishtailing back and forth across the channel, kind of like doing a snowplow on skis. With only 400 feet to work with though, it's not a lot of help.

An outbound container ship is approaching and her pilot is freaking at my maneuvers. I tell him I'll hold her as far right as I can when we meet and to keep on coming. I pull the tug hard outside the channel to keep the barge up as much as I can and it seems to be working. The container ship slides by about 25 feet away, just a massive black steel cliff. I've already pissed my pants so many times in the last hour, I'm empty.

I look back and now the barge is sideways, half in and half out of the channel. The only reason she's not already aground is that we already dropped the load in Tampa so she's riding light. *Behave, you bastard!* As soon as the container ship clears, I throw the wheel hard left and pull for the opposite side of the channel. The barge is still smoking along but is now sideways to the tug. "Goddamn you Ralph," I mutter.

I slam the throttle forward to goose her back in line, and I see one of the channel markers coming up. It's a flashing light mounted high in the air on a crib of 20 or 30 telephone pole-size wooden posts, so a fairly substantial structure. Still sideways, the barge is heading right for it. There is absolutely nothing I can do except watch in horror as ponderously, and with no sound that I can hear, she mows that light right down. Blinking cheerfully one second, simply gone the next. *Sonofabitch.*

That was an interesting call to the Coast Guard: "Uh, hey guys, ya know all those lights you have out in Mobile Bay? I hate to tell you this, but now you got one less."

We went blowing by the junction a full two hours ahead of the meet-up. That's bad news, as now we have to go all the way into the Mobile inner harbor before we can turn this beast around, and that's no treat. Good news is my watch is almost over and I get to hand it over to Ralph with the inner harbor lights twinkling in the front window. He comes up and about shits.

I said, "Mornin', cuz…we be in downtown Mobile…tide took me right past the junction early, just like I thought…there's a ton of traffic headin' your way…happy motorin'." And off to my rack I stumble. I'm thinking, *Poor Ralph's gonna be late for his date.*

With the boomtown atmosphere in Theodore you couldn't swing a cat without hitting a prostitute, or "Harbor Queen." They were everywhere. Even walking up the street to mail a letter forced you to dodge a gauntlet of H.Q.'s waiting outside the dock gates. "Hey there, Shugah. Y'all wanna date?" "Ah, no thanks Darlin'. I gotta get back to the boat." No point in being rude. They were mainly decent gals with a tough job.

Bob *loved* Harbor Queens. Or as he insisted we call them, "escorts." Bob was not a classically handsome man, and pretty much lived on the boats 11 months a year. Not only did he not have time for a real relationship, some woman would have taken advantage of his absence and good nature, and cleaned him out. Escorts were perfect for Bob.

Bob didn't just hire escorts willy-nilly. When he found one he liked, he kept her around for a while and treated her like gold. The gals appreciated it and reciprocated his good intentions. In Theodore, his main professional squeeze was a woman named Taylor. Taylor was a beautiful, self-employed businesswoman. After whatever hijinks she and Bob performed in his room, she would hang out in the galley, drink coffee and bullshit with us. She was smart, witty and had a great sense of humor. We all thought the world of her.

One day I had an idea.

When we had a crew change, most of the guys flew somewhere. The best airport to use was in Pensacola, a two-hour cab ride away. The guy would take a cab to P-Cola, get a room at company expense, and fly out in the morning. Both going and coming.

I was responsible for handling the tug's cash. We carried a $7000 bank as we often had to pay for incidentals on the spot. When I got low I would contact

Janet in the Cleveland office and she would FedEx me another 7K—in cash—in a big fat FedEx envelope. A lot of 10's, and 20's, and a few 50's. Big thick envelope. I kept immaculate records, using a little creative accounting now and then only to benefit the boat, but I could account for every dime.

As much money as the company wasted on tugs to pull us off the sandbars, they were stingy about crew creature comforts. They did allow $150 for cab fare to get change crew to Pensacola where they would go on receipted travel expenses, no questions asked. The buck fifty came out of my bank.

Taylor had a brand new Jeep Grand Cherokee, a cell phone, and a computer. Like I said, she was a sharp, self-employed businesswoman. One evening we were sitting around the galley, shootin' the shit after she screwed Bob into a coma, and I threw out a question: "Say, Taylor, you know we're always sending guys to P-Cola to catch flights. What would you charge me to take over the transports? Could you do it for $100? I'll give you a hundie for the trip but you can make any deals you want with the guys on the way to the airport. They get a nice hotel over there and an expense account for dinner—no reason they can't feed you too. Give me a receipt for $150 and I can use the extra bucks to buy the crew a premium movie package or a crawfish dinner now and then. Of course we'll invite you."

She thought for about two seconds. "Yeah, that could work. Bob always gives me a few days' notice, and I know you guys would be flexible if I was busy and a couple hours late…Sure, I'm in. I might have to take care of Bob first though."

"Oh, hell yeah, that goes without sayin'. No problem there."

So the rest of the time I was there—and for who knows how long after I left—Taylor was our official taxi. And from the reports I heard from the guys, she did well with the crew of the *Mohawk*. I drilled into their heads to "be gentlemen, be classy, don't forget to tip." She would show up looking hot and smelling good, with a cooler full of iced beer—each guy's preference.

They couldn't dive over the rail and get in her Jeep fast enough. The crew was *thrilled* with our new driver. I was really pleased by how it all worked out and we got a major upgrade to our TV sports package! Plus the guys treated me like a god! There were no discipline issues on the *'Hawk.*

As many thrills as there were going and coming in Mobile Bay and on the other end in Tampa Bay, the really big heart-stoppers were out in the Gulf of Mexico during our transits, or out "on the salt," as the Cajuns would say.

The only good thing was that our horror show of a barge was "on the string" and as far back as we could get her. Problem was, she was so heavy that even a quarter mile back, she still controlled the motion of the tug. Instead of the tug sailing freely over the big waves, the weight of the tow cable held the stern down and the tug would take the punch of a big sea right in the face. Again and again, all the way across the Gulf, which was usually at least a three-day trip.

Weather in the Gulf could go from blazing sunshine and calm seas to a raging blow in a matter of hours. You could see it coming. And the *Mohawk* was a terrible sea boat. She was so low that the bow would bury itself in an oncoming wave and the whole wheelhouse would be underwater for a moment. It would be light then dark green, light then dark green. That was during the day.

At night it would be dark then black, dark then black. It was a little unnerving. I always wondered when the windows would cave in. I knew we were in deep shit one night when we were beating into huge seas. At one point the bow was buried in an oncoming wave and I looked out the wheelhouse window at a porpoise flashing by higher than my head. We were farther under water than he was.

The real test of a Gulf boat was how she would handle hurricanes. From the first day we were down there, local tug guys kept asking where were our storm shutters? Even giant seagoing tugs had steel shutters with narrow viewing slits they dropped over the wheelhouse windows in a hurricane. We had no such thing on the *Mohawk*. Just lots of glass.

The guys in Theodore were also curious about our hurricane plan, and their concern prompted my own. Inquiring about that to the home office in Cleveland received the response, "Don't worry, we'll just send *Mohawk* to ride it out at sea." Granted, that's what the real big boats do. The idea is to dodge the incoming storm surge, and as far as that goes, it's a proven concept. But the smaller tugs, crew boats and fishing boats all went up the river past Mobile, tied off to trees on the bank, got the hell off the boat, and ran 20 miles inland to wait it out. Telling them we planned to ride through it offshore brought low whistles and head shakes. "In *that* boat? Good luck, cuz…better you than me." Not a ringing endorsement.

In August, I was off on vacation and preparing to return to the 'Hawk. Watching the Weather Channel, every hour at 10 minutes to the hour was a segment called Tropical Forecast. Sitting at home in Indian River, Michigan, I watched a hurricane named Isidore developing and heading right for Mobile. I got a call from the office in Cleveland wanting me to cut my vacation short and get down to Mobile pronto as they were preparing to send *Mohawk* to ride through the storm way out on the salt. I thought for about a second and said, "Ya know, I don't think I wanna do that. Guess you better find another mate.

No hard feelings, it's been fun."

I made a couple calls and was back on a Great Lakes ore boat days later with the best tan on Lake Superior.

I heard from the guys a few weeks later. They said they almost lost the boat riding out that hurricane. The *Hawk* suffered a lot of damage and scared the living hell out of the whole crew. One engine crapped out, they sprung a leak, and were down to only one pump. Two wheelhouse windows were broken. Three guys quit as soon as they returned to the dock.

Sometimes, like a smart rat, you just have to know when to jump ship.

4

Typhoon Ivy

The word used to describe a severe, rotating storm varies depending on where one occurs. In the Atlantic Ocean they are hurricanes. In the Southern Ocean such a weather phenomenon is labeled a cyclone. In the Pacific Ocean, it's a typhoon. No matter what title they spin under, they describe the same thing: an incredibly destructive weather event.

In October of 1977, in the warm waters of the Western Pacific Ocean, a tropical depression formed, increasing to tropical storm status and quickly becoming a full-blown typhoon. This was a named storm designated Typhoon Ivy.

Typhoon Ivy, October 1977, near Marcus Island,
1100 miles southeast of Tokyo.

With sustained winds in excess of 100 mph, Ivy stayed at sea, sparing mainland communities her damage. But her wrath would be felt hundreds of miles in the distance.

Over 3000 miles away in the tiny coastal village of Sitka, Alaska, the Coast Guard cutter *Clover* (WLB-292) was preparing to depart for an extended ocean voyage.

Every two years, Coast Guard vessels were required to report to a U.S. Navy facility to undergo "refresher training," abbreviated as "REFTRA" and pronounced "Ref-tray." Although a separate service, in time of war the Coast Guard operated as a part of the Navy. So it was necessary to train and remain current in Naval procedures, wartime operations and shipboard emergency response.

East Coast boats trained with the Navy in Norfolk, Virginia or Guantanamo Bay (Gitmo) Cuba, while West Coast ships went to San Diego or Pearl Harbor, Hawaii. Either would be quite a journey for the *Clover*. We were ordered to proceed to Pearl Harbor.

Even though the training would be time-consuming and very intense, the crew of the *Clover* was excited by the prospect of spending time in Hawaii, especially when compared to the consistently gloomy fall weather of Southeast Alaska. We were thinking about swaying palms and hula girls, with not much thought given to an October passage across the North Pacific Ocean.

USCGC Clover {wlb-292}

The *Clover* was feeling and looking her age. A 180-foot buoy tender built in 1942 by Zenith Dock and Dredge in Duluth, Minnesota, she was 35 years old and the salt water was taking a toll on her hull and systems. She saw duty in the Aleutians in WW2. After the war she worked herself all over the world doing what she was built to do: tending buoys and supplying far-flung light stations with water and fuel. She was a seaworthy design but not very comfortable for the crew, due to her relatively stubby lines and rounded hull. As the boys often said, "She would roll like a pig on a gallon of dew."

As Typhoon Ivy tracked her way across the deserted wastes of the Pacific Ocean, her winds were having a huge effect on the seas. Blasting across miles of ocean in a northeast direction, the winds were howling straight at Alaska. Seas were building to monstrous size and beginning to batter the Alaskan coast.

Typhoon Ivy would eventually blow herself out, but her effects were far-reaching. The vicious winds and huge seas she spawned could continue for weeks.

As departure day neared for the *Clover*, the captain was watching the coming storm. It looked like it might be a tough crossing but these REFTRA commitments were made years in advance and no captain wanted to tell the admiral up in the district office he couldn't make his training dates. No captain who ever expected to be promoted, that is. So plans for our departure continued unchecked.

The storm hit Sitka with a fury the night before we were scheduled to go. It was so bad the crew fully expected our departure would be delayed. We were all surprised when we got word we would leave the next morning. An uneasy feeling began to filter through the ship. We didn't give a rat's ass if we disappointed the admiral. Nobody was looking forward to a multiday ass-kicking just so our captain could get another stripe.

We dropped our lines at daybreak and headed west, but with the heavy cloud cover it was so dark you couldn't tell it was morning. Leaving the protection of the harbor, the *Clover* found herself in the teeth of a raging sea.

Still in the relatively protected waters of Sitka Sound, the ship was being tossed around like a toy. It was impossible to tell the difference between wind-driven sleet streaking the windows and the crushing tons of heavy spray lashing across the boat. No one could stand up without clinging to a support. Staggering down a passage way required stepping on the walls as the ship rolled violently from side to side. So much water and foam was flying through the air that the radar was useless. The LORAN (LOng Range Aid to Navigation) receiver was also damaged and inoperative. Chugging blindly out to sea, we were just guessing, or "Ded Reckoning," where we were. Deduced Reckoning is an estimated position calculated by projecting course steered, ship's speed and any wind/current effects.

The crew was taking a severe beating. Many of the guys were vomiting and that sharp, tangy smell permeated the bridge, bringing new guests to the party all the time.

Neb the FNG, or "Fucking New Guy," from Nebraska, was down on the deck and puking constantly. Serious soul-tearing retching. In between heaves you could hear him sobbing in agony and terror. There are very few oceans in Nebraska and it was apparent his recruiter had been less than truthful with young Neb: "It's the *Coast* Guard, Son. We just work the beach." *Ha ha...sure.* Today we couldn't see the beach with binoculars.

Eight hours underway and everyone's exhausted from just hanging on. We can't confirm but we think we have to be out past Biorka Island and into the

Gulf of Alaska by now. After pounding away all day, we should be 80 or 90 miles down the track.

Neb was beginning to throw up blood and "Doc," our hospital corpsman, was seriously concerned.

Cap was making a decision on what to do about Neb when a new emergency arises. One of the engineers took a digger down an engine-room ladder and had a broken shoulder. A helicopter medevac is impossible so the captain has no choice but to turn around. We get a break in the storm, and there off to port is the light flashing on Biorka Island. I'm stunned. All day and we've only made 22 miles.

"How far is Hawaii?" Bobby the helmsman ("Night Creature") whispers to me. I grimace from behind the chart table. "It's 3000 miles, bro."

He pales. "Oh my God."

I agree. "Ya got that right, Creature, we're fucked."

We take a 50-degree lean turning around, and guys go flying across the wheelhouse, piling up in the corner along with coffee cups, charts and Creature's garbage bag of puke. *Clover's* a stout sea boat though, and she takes it in stride. She slowly rights herself, we all get back on our feet, and with the weather now behind us pushing, we're headed back to town like a missile. We finally make the harbor and the sudden calm is surreal. The battered crew tie the boat up, and the whole gang charges off to the Pioneer Bar. We figured the trip was cancelled. We wanted it to be. It had to be. Screw the palm trees and hula girls. *Gimme another beer.*

Imagine our hungover shock the next morning when the ships speaker blared out: NOW PREPARE TO GET UNDERWAY…SET THE SPECIAL SEA DETAIL. Doug ("Popeye"), the master at arms, comes through the berthing space shaking out the late sleepers and we ask him, "Are you shittin' us? We're going again?"

"Yup, that we are…so saddle up, bitches." *Aw, damn.*

We clear the harbor and head her seaward into more of the same. It's Yesterday 2.0. We're just blindly beating into the weather and getting stomped. This time we pound out past Biorka and keep going. Now we're in the Gulf of Alaska, the big water, as the ship's speaker warns: NOW ALL HANDS… STANDBY FOR HEAVY ROLLS. *Duh, really? Ya think?*

Almost immediately we sail into a foaming hell. Seas were building steadily and were 45-50 footers with breaking white foam along the crests. Winds clocking 75 mph. Force 12 on the Beaufort Sea State Scale.

The *Clover* would climb almost vertically up one monster and be launched into space as the wave passed underneath, free falling into the dark trough like she was dropping into an elevator shaft. The ship would bottom out with a bone rattling BOOOOM and shake like a wet dog. The noise was incredible. The next wave would break over the top of us and the ship would actually punch through the center of the wall, the wheelhouse windows totally under and covered in green water as we staggered *through* the wave and out the other side.

Only to climb...drop...punch through again...climb...drop...punch through. All the while we're rolling, jerking, slamming and flying through the air inside the ship with our stomachs dropping from throat to feet and back again.

BEAUFORT FORCE 12
WIND SPEED: 64 KNOTS

SEA: SEA COMPLETELY WHITE WITH DRIVING SPRAY,
VISIBILITY VERY SERIOUSLY AFFECTED. THE
AIR IS FILLED WITH FOAM AND SPRAY

As the ship flew over a wave, the propeller would come out of the water and start to spin free with a shrill rising scream. When we dropped into the trough and the screw bit deep, the engine would slow as it struggled to catch up with itself. It would almost stop and then gradually pick up speed, rising to a shrieking crescendo again as we went airborne off the next wave, before going back under and again struggle to keep turning.

Clinging to our racks, desperately trying not to get flung out on the deck, our hearts were beating along with the engine. "Come on, baby...come on, baby...let's go...come on...come-on come-on come-on...whew...thank you, Jesus." And repeat, ad infinitum.

There was no reprieve, day after day after day. Everybody was puking until they were too exhausted to puke anymore. Then they'd lay in the rack dry heaving or just wishing for death. To this day I laugh when some summer sailor thumps his chest and brags, "I don't get seasick!" *Is that right, Buttercup?* You just told me you haven't been in bad enough weather yet.

Ensign Johnson standing watch while praying for a quick death.

The ship was taking a terrible thrashing and her weaknesses were beginning to show. Her wiring was the old stuff with the cloth covering, and as the ship writhed and pounded these rubbed together and, with the friction, started catching fire. It was terrifying to be isolated on a ship, miles offshore, fighting through a typhoon and hear the loudspeaker: NOW THIS IS NOT A DRILL...THIS IS NOT A DRILL...FIRE FIRE FIRE, FIRE IN THE ENGINE SPACE...ALL HANDS PROVIDE."

Everyone flies out of their racks—nobody had dared to get undressed anyway—stumbling, and in some cases crawling, to their emergency stations, providing all the equipment to fight the fire. We put the fires out as fast as we could, but over the course of the journey that call froze our blood seven more times.

Even worse was the specter of a steering casualty. If we lost steering we were dead. That simple. No way could we survive these seas with a frozen rudder. When this panicked call actually came, I really thought we were done. By this point I didn't even care. NOW THIS IS NOT A DRILL...THIS IS NOT A DRILL...STEERING CASUALTY STEERING CASUALTY STEERING CASUALTY...STAND BY AFTER STEERING ON THE DOUBLE.

Crawling up the ladder on all fours, I went tearing aft to my station at the emergency wheel in the After Steering compartment. I got there at the same time as an engineer and we almost crashed our heads together grabbing the wheel. We both hung on as the ship dropped through yet another torturous series of waves. We kept the wheel steady for what seemed forever, but was really only minutes, before the problem was found and quickly lashed together. Back to my rack, bouncing from bulkhead to bulkhead and jacked out of my skull with adrenaline, I wondered if I would ever be able to sleep again.

We had stripped the weather decks of life-rings, tools, flags, and anything that might blow loose or be washed away, stowing everything in an inside gear locker. Included in this pile of loose equipment was a large smoke pot, a signaling device usually attached to a life-ring to aid in spotting a man overboard. It put out thick clouds of red smoke and lasted for at least 30 seconds. Pulling a ring located on top of the device activated it, and once triggered it could not be shut off.

Slipping on a puddle of vomit, one of the deckies opened the locker to grab a swab. It was stuck on something so he gave it a hard jerk. Unfortunately it was caught on the activation ring and when he pulled on the swab the ring came out and activated the smoke bomb.

With a loud pop and a nasty hiss the galley immediately filled with choking red smoke. Guys were scattering like cockroaches in the sunlight but there was no place to run. People were flat on the floor sucking at any fresh air they could find. It was a long thirty seconds. Of course the portholes and hatches were all dogged down tight so there was nowhere for the smoke to go.

Jack, the chief bos'n, desperately threw open a hatch (door) leading to the buoy deck. The vestibule was immediately filled with icy salt water as he was knocked backwards off his feet, slamming into the bulkhead (wall). Crew scrambled to secure the slamming hatch and wrestle it closed. Water was just pouring in. Decks awash now, the guys braced themselves as the ship continued its crashing ride. Opening the door as we went airborne, a little smoke could be vented out before the ship dropped into the trough and the door had to be slammed closed. Open, close…open, close…open, close. After much screaming, yelling and running around, enough smoke was vented to allow fairly normal breathing. We all tasted that smoke for days.

Dale, the guy who set off the bomb, was flat on his back, sliding around in the puddle he initially went to clean up. He was red head to toe, coated with residue from the smoke, and his eyes were bugging out of his head.

I skidded past him on the way up to my watch in the wheelhouse. Might as well laugh about it. "Nice job, Dale…good equipment test." I gave him a thumbs up. He just lay there, gulping air like a fish out of water and didn't say a word. The middle finger of his right hand slowly came up in acknowledgment.

A trip that should have taken 9 days took 14. Our beating continued unabated for 12 of them. I had serious doubts we would live through it, but you can only be terrified for so long and then it gets tiresome. My philosophy was: If we were going to sink, I wished it had been at the beginning of the trip instead of at the end. *Why suffer for days if you're gonna die anyway?* Once you face the fact that there is absolutely nothing you can do except hang on and operate the boat as best you can, fear evaporates. The pain continues though.

The last two days, the winds and the seas dropped and the sun came out. Crew came stumbling into the sunlight, eyes burning in the unaccustomed glare. We were filthy, still in the same clothes we had been wearing for days. The smell of dirty bodies, old puke, spoiled food and sewage wafted through the boat. We paid no attention to little things like that.

The ship was trashed. Salt water rushed back and forth throughout the lower decks and broken crockery crunched underfoot. On deck, one of the work boats had jumped the cradle and needed repair. The signal flag box on the upper deck was soaked and all the flags were a soggy mess. The cover on the anchor was just gone. Moving like zombies, we started to put things right.

We finally rolled into the Sand Island Coast Guard Base in Honolulu at 7:00 p.m. on a beautiful tropical evening. Palm trees were swaying but there were no hula girls to be seen. A mangy dog listlessly lifted his leg on a dockside garbage can. But it was a *Hawaiian* dog!

As soon as the ship tied up, crew began dazedly walking down the gangway to stand silently on the pier. Several guys lay down flat on the warm asphalt and I saw two crewmen kissing the pavement.

There was an enlisted club right on the dock and we all headed in, officers and crew together. Nobody said much, just grabbed a beer and chugged it down. It stayed quiet for a half hour, guys just drinking and thinking, grateful to still be alive. After some time passed, conversations started.

"Man, do you remember that one hit we took?"

"Whadya mean, *one*??"

"How about those fires?" an engineer said.

"Man, that steering casualty almost made me piss my pants." And the cook added, "Can you believe Dale set off that smoke bomb?"

Guys are laughing now. More beers. The club refused to take our money. We later found out the captain had paid for everything. We guessed he could have that other stripe after all.

Morning dawned on a quiet ship. Cooks moved stiffly around in the galley ready to prepare breakfast, but there were few takers. Guys were sprawled out all over the boat, some passed out still drunk and many just too whipped to move. Gradually though, the *Clover* started to come back to life.

Clover crew drying signal flags.

The crew got rested and calmed down some. Damage around the ship was patched up. We moved over to our new berth in Pearl Harbor and checked in with the Navy Fleet Training Group. *We're here for training; let's get this over with.*

But first we had a duty to perform.

When a visiting ship comes to Pearl Harbor, at some point in their stay it is traditional to "render honors" to the *Battleship Arizona*, still resting beneath the harbor with the remains of 1000 crewmen entombed inside.

The United States Coast Guard cutter *Clover* (WLB-292), the "Pride of Sitka, Alaska," sparkling clean with all flags flying, cruised slowly past the Arizona memorial. Officers and crew in dress uniforms lined up along the sides in neat rows, called "manning the rail."

Photo courtesy of U.S. Navy Brochure: *Manning the Rail: A U.S. Navy Tradition*

Navy crew "manning the rail" at the Arizona memorial.

As we passed the *Arizona*, the call came on the deck speakers: ATTENTION ON DECK...HAAAND saaaLUTE ! Fifty-six arms come up as one, and the flag on the mast is dipped in honor. It was a surprisingly emotional moment. My dad joined the Navy on December 6, 1941. He spent most of WW2 as a radio operator on a submarine chaser based in Hawaii. At that moment, I felt a connection run through me like an electric current.

REAAADY...HUUH! With a snap, our arms come down, and we sail on through the harbor with lumps in more than a few throats, to begin our training.

Training went well and we learned a lot. Once, however, after eight straight hours on the wheel, I did miss a Simon Says-type command and turned left instead of right, sailing us right into an imaginary minefield. Fortunately, it wasn't real and we all got a laugh out if it. I asked the captain, "Since we're blown up, could I please go hit my rack?" I couldn't forget it though. And never in 40-odd years did I made a mistake like that again, no matter how tired or stressed I was. That's the purpose of training.

When it was time to depart and sail back to Sitka, we all had knots in our guts anticipating the ordeal that may again be waiting for us out on the salt. But the trip back was uneventful, almost pleasant. Seven crewmembers went

AWOL (Absent WithOut Leave) in Honolulu though, because they couldn't face a repeat of our trip down. They waited until the ship was out of helicopter range and then checked in at the base. They all got an extra week in Hawaii before they were flown back to Alaska, facing shipboard restrictions and small fines. But every one of the "Clover 7" said it was worth it.

Clover at Sand Island Coast Guard Base in Honolulu, Hawaii.

5

Dark and Stormy Nights

Over the years there were many isolated incidents that I personally found funny or exciting. These brief blips in time wouldn't stand alone as a long story themselves, but are still good tales to tell.

NOW THIS IS NOT A DRILL
On the *Medusa Conquest/Susan W. Hannah*

The *Medusa Conquest* was the barge portion of an ATB unit, which stands for Articulated Tug and Barge. There was a V-shaped notch cut in the stern of the barge, and a tugboat was mated to the notch, hooked to the barge with "pins." This allowed the stern of the tug to rise and fall with the seas, but connected the pair as a single unit.

She was pushed around the Lakes by the Hannah Marine Corporation tug, *Susan W. Hannah*. (Hannah Marine Corporation was owned by movie actress Darryl Hannah's daddy.) The crew lived on the tug but had easy access to the barge. This enabled us to step up on the barge underway to perform maintenance and make safety rounds. Plus it made it possible to get some distance from the other idiots on the tug when the claustrophobic conditions became too intense.

Brad was the captain and I was sailing as mate. He was a fun guy to work with, a total professional and very laid back. I always enjoyed my time on the *Susan W* with him.

We were unloading in Owen Sound, Ontario, business as usual, when the big generator that ran the unloading system on the barge caught fire. This was a sharp crew. They were right on it and had the fire out almost immediately. They started up the standby generator and the unload proceeded with only a minor hiccup.

Brad was back on the tug asleep. The fire was out and damage was slight but he was the captain and I had to inform him ASAP. Back to the tug I go, thinking hard on the way about just how to accomplish this with as little initial trauma to Brad as possible. Fire is one of the most serious situations you can encounter on a ship, just one step below actually sinking. The word alone scares the living shit out of mariners.

Brad was a very sound sleeper. I always woke him up by handing him a cup of coffee. I would make him take it in his hand as I knew if I set it on his desk he would roll over and go back to sleep.

Thinking, that's as good a place as any to start, I got a cup of coffee, knocked lightly and opened his door. "Brad…Brad…hey Brad…wakey wakey," I crooned in as gentle a voice as I could manage.

"Huh? Huh…Wha' times it?" he said as he groggily sat up, automatically reaching for the coffee.

OK, here we go.

"Now Brad, everything's *fine*, we're still pumping off, and I repeat…*all's well now*…but…we had a fire on the barge," I try to say easily and calmly, adding in a rush of words, "It's out, it's out, we got it…"

The only word Brad heard was "fire."

"A FIRE?!! WHATS ON FIRE?!" He jumps up, whacking his head on the edge of the upper bunk and dumping hot coffee on his legs. "OWWWWW, SONOFABITCH! A FIRE??"

He's standing up now wearing only his baggy boxers, just wild-eyed and alternately rubbing his head and his leg. He starts hopping around trying to get his pants on, still shouting questions.

"Brad, Brad…easy man. It's OK…we got it out…the chief says there's not a lot of damage. I'm just letting you know. I hated to wake you with the news but you know I had to tell you. I tried not ta scare ya," I said.

He stops and stares at me with one leg in his pants. His voice cracking, he croaks out, "Well…YOU FAILED!!"

We had a good laugh about it later. I asked him if there was any possible way to wake up a captain and tell him his ship was on fire without scaring the piss out of him. He had to agree there probably wasn't.

"And don't forget, Brad, I did bring you coffee!"

"Yeah right, thanks. My legs enjoyed it," he said.

"You're welcome, brother.

Southern Comfort
Also on the *Susan W. Hannah*

Dave was one of the deckhands, and hailed from Kentucky. He wore his nickname "Hillbilly" as proudly as his denim bib-tops. (He called his bibbers a "Kentucky tuxedo.") A good guy, slow talking with a thick southern drawl, there was never a doubt who you were talking to when Dave had the radio.

We loaded cement in Charlevoix, Michigan and since I lived in Indian River, I liked to run home now and then. Sometimes it worked out that I was off watch, but more often I had to work. It was allowed to get another crew member to "standby" for you and cover your watch. This involved outright bribery on a sliding scale depending on how bad you wanted off and how mercenary the other guy was feeling.

Ideally I could make a deal with a guy who lived down south near one of our unload ports. He would take my watches in Charlevoix and I would take his down south. That way no money changed hands and it was a straightforward deal.

This time, I really needed to get home and was begging someone to swap a watch with me. Finally Dave said he would do it, with the standard agreement that I would take a watch for him later.

OK, good deal. Home I went.

Later, back out on the lake, I approach Dave and said, "Stay in bed tonight, I got your midwatch."

"Ohhh nooo," he drawled. "Ah'm saaavin' it."

This wasn't the way it was supposed to work. Usually you paid a guy back as soon as you could after we left port. But he did bail me out so I agreed he had one in the bank.

Months go by. I know Dave hasn't forgotten because often while sitting around the galley he would grin and drawl, "Ah'm saaavin'' it."

"Jesus, Dave, let me square it already."

"Nope. Ah'll letcha know."

Late November, we're pulling in to unload in Milwaukee. It was just a hideous night. Freezing cold. Black as the inside of a boot. Rain/sleet blowing in sideways. Barge rocking and rolling at the dock with ice-cold spray blasting in sheets across the deck. It was a bitch getting tied up. I had been called out on overtime for the tie-up and was grateful to get off the deck and back into my warm, snuggy rack.

Sighing in contentment, I was just about to close my eyes when the door opened and Dave burst in.

"Tah-nahts the naht," he grins gleefully.

"Are you freakin' *kiddin'* me Dave, you soulless bastard."

"Nope, you got'er ta-naht." He was practically dancing with joy.

Well, I do owe the guy, so no whining. Back into my cold clammy gear I climb and out to one of the most wretched nights of my life. Not only did I have to stand Dave's watch, but my own rolled right in behind it at 0400, so I got a double dose: eight straight hours of absolute misery.

At breakfast Dave was in his glory. As each crewmember stumbled in to eat, Dave would crow, "Ah got Lonnie. Ah got'm gooooood."

I couldn't help but laugh.

"That you did, Hillbilly, you Appalachian reject. Well played."

Hit The Road, Jack
On the *Undaunted*

I was working out of Ludington, Michigan for Pere Marquette Shipping on the tug *Undaunted*, pushing an open-deck, bulk-commodity barge, the *Pere Marquette 41*.

The *Undaunted* was a 1945-vintage tug that had gone through many renovations in the intervening years. She spent WW2 in the Pacific and was used to tow battle-damaged Navy ships into port. Since she carried armaments back then, she was designated an "Attack Tug," which is really a contradiction in terms, but still pretty cool.

The captain's name was Tim, in his mid-50s, and he was a wizened little gnome of a guy. He reminded me of Popeye. Tim had been a tugboat man since he could walk and had absolutely not one politically correct bone in his body.

Tim "called 'em as he see'd 'em" and if you didn't like it, as he was fond of saying, "Tuff titty, amigo."

Tim was on his third wife, this one a former "dancer" named Roxy he met at Studio 10, the infamous strip club on the banks of the St. Marys River in Soo, Ontario. Actually, the crew all thought he hit the jackpot with Roxy. She was pretty cool and seemed to really love Tim, in spite of his abrasive personality. I think she knocked off a few of his rough edges.

He liked me and we got along well. I was a reliable navigator, and as he told me, "At least I can get some sleep when you're up there." That was extremely high praise from a tough nut like Tim.

As first mate, I ran the crew during loading and unloading ops. The Merchant Marine isn't like the Navy so there is a certain amount of lip and crap you take from those hard-ass crews. But if you treat the guys well, there is generally mutual respect and things operate with a minimum of bullshit.

We got a new deckhand from Manitowac, Wisconsin named Harold, a big fat kid around 22 years old. A real mouthy shitbird right off the bat. I don't know where he thought he was. First watch working on deck I gave him a simple order and he responded very rude and sarcastic, almost refusing to do what I asked.

Hmmm. What's this idiot's deal? I wonder, kind of shrugging it off.

His disrespectful and downright insulting attitude continues through the trip though, and I've had enough. I went through the whole gamut of first mate tricks, from reasoning to understanding to outright yelling and threats of bodily violence. Now I'm hunting this clown for every dirty job I can find, but he is still being a supreme asshole. He's a terrible worker too, so there is nothing in his favor. I'm not complaining to anybody though. This is part of the job and I'm dealing with it, but word gets around to Tim.

We're pulling into Muskegon and Tim calls me on the radio. "Hey kid, soon as we're tied off come up to the wheelhouse. I got a present for ya."

"Roger that boss, be right up."

I get up to the wheelhouse and Tim's grinning. "Watch this" he says. "Happy Birthday." *Hmmm, it's not my birthday. What's up?* Cap calls down to the galley and tells the cook to send Harold up.

Harold comes puffing up the ladder to the wheelhouse. Tim winks at me, turns and sneers at Harold. "Pack ur shit, doughboy, ur through."

The look on that dickwad's face was priceless. Payback for all the crap he had shoveled my way. He was shocked. *His mama promised he was special.*

I gleefully pointed back down the ladder, "You heard the cap, numbnuts. Off ya go now."

He looks back at Tim, hoping for a reprieve and gets: "Tuff titty amigo, bye-bye."

He was *triple* fired. So long, farewell, adios.

I was delighted. You just don't see that anymore, at least not on the boats: A bad employee actually let go. The office usually won't allow it. Too afraid of a lawsuit.

Tim didn't care. As he put it, "Ya have a bad tooth, ya yank it."

Political correctness is overrated.

I Learn Some Norwegian
On the M/V *Tustumena*

I was brand new working for the State of Alaska Ferry System. The M/V *Tustumena* was my first ship with them. I was hired as an AB, or able seaman, a rating responsible for steering the ship in docking and other tight situations, and doing other deck work. I had been steering ships for six years already and after four years in the Coast Guard, was way past experienced. I definitely knew what I was doing.

Usually helm commands were begun by the pilot saying something like "left (or right) 15." It meant spin the wheel and move the rudder 15 degrees to start a turn on a prescribed arc. Obviously, fewer degrees would carve a wider arc, more degrees on the rudder would make a tighter turn. When the desired course was approaching, the helmsman would "shift" the rudder the opposite direction to "check" or slow the swing. But you had to know what the new course was before you could "meet her" and steady on the new course.

When the ship would start turning, there was an audible device connected to the gyro compass called a "tattletale." This made a loud clicking sound, usually four times in one degree, so a click for every quarter degree of movement. This kept everyone in the wheelhouse aware of the ship moving right or left and how fast. As the rate of turn increased, the tattletale would start clicking faster. During a normal at-sea watch, steady on a given course and with a good helmsman, the tattletale would only sound off now and then. It would be like click…minutes pass…click…more minutes…click/click…click and so on, as the helmsman made minor adjustments to keep the ship on course.

So we are coming into Homer, Alaska. I'm on the wheel and cruising right along. The ship enters Kachemak Bay on a straight track, and then when it gets near the dock needs to make a hard left turn to line it up.

The first mate in the front window (piloting) is a native of Norway, named Ole, and speaks with a thick Norwegian accent. He turns to me and says, "Left 15." *No prob, left 15 it is*, and we start turning to port. Tattletale starts clicking and picks up speed. Still OK, business as usual. Ole looks over his shoulder and spits out: "DOONORT."

"What?" I said.

"DOONORT," he says again.

By this time we are cranking hard to the left and the tattletale is really ripping. It sounds like a zipper. I'm waiting for him to give me a course to steady up on, normally a 3 digit number from 000 degrees to 360 degrees, indicating what to steer, but I'm not getting it.

"Jesus, Mate, I don't know what you want!" I'm practically yelling now. I'm thinking, *For God's sake, give me a course!!*

He's screaming now too because we're just smokin' around the corner.

"DOONORT DOONORT DOONORT." I am at a loss, just hangin' on to the wheel and wondering where the hell we're gonna end up parkin' this bucket, when the captain turns out of his chair, laughing, and says, "He wants you to steer triple zero." 000 Degrees.

DOONORT? DUE NORTH? WTF? *Are you shittin' me?* I immediately throw hard opposite rudder on and she starts to check up, slowing down. Ole's looking wild and my heart's in my throat. I get her stopped, heading back on course, and we all take a breath.

Ole forgot he wasn't on a Norwegian boat and that American helm commands are given in degrees. I could have even handled that if it wasn't so unexpected, and if he wasn't talking like he had a mouthful of lefsa, lutefisk, or some other Scandinavian soul food.

As most Merchant Marine near misses go, we all had a big laugh afterwards. *Ha ha...yeah, we almost died...wasn't that a hoot...I'll go change my drawers and then let's have coffee.*

Answered Prayers
On the Mackinac Island Ferry, *Chippewa*

As the Mackinac Island "traditional" ferries went, they never ran out of fuel. For one thing the tanks were huge. For another, the fuel trucks topped them off so often they never had a chance to run very low. Because of this there was always a couple feet of sludge left in the bottom of the tanks that never got run out.

This wasn't a problem unless it was a rough day and the tanks hadn't been fully topped off. Then the rocking motion of the boat churned up the tanks and sent a bunch of crud into the fuel filters. At times, this would completely plug the filter causing one of the engines to start laboring from lack of fuel and then choke out entirely. While it was a pain in the ass, it wasn't serious, as we had two engines and would just change out the filters during the next port stop.

Coming back from the Island one afternoon with a light load of passengers, it was bouncing around pretty good. As I lined up for the approach to the St. Ignace dock, I heard one of the engines sputter and die. Guessing the probable cause, I wasn't concerned.

On a big twin-screw ship the props turn in opposite directions, so when you come in on one engine you need to know which one you have. Adjustments must be made for the boat now setting one way or the other, depending on which direction your single prop is turning. It changes the necessary angle of approach to the dock. It's not a big deal, but your line-up does change.

I made an announcement on the loudspeaker that "nothing to be concerned about folks, but one of my engines just tripped off the line. I'll be doing a donut here in the harbor to line myself up better for a one-engine approach."

No biggie. *Easy peasy.* Happens all the time.

We made the dock and tied up with no problems. Then one of the deckhands stuck his head in the wheelhouse, "Hey Cap, you might wanna come down and see this."

I went down to the main deck and there I saw a family group of eight or nine folks, young children up to Grandma and Grandpa. They were all wearing bright orange life jackets they had broken out from the emergency lockers and were tightly clustered together in a huddle, clinging to each other, crying and praying loudly.

I was approaching the fear stricken group when Grandma looked up and saw me. Panic stricken she shouted, "What are *you* doing down here? Who's driving the *boat*"? Like she thought I was there to abandon ship.

"Ahh, easy there, Ma'am. Look out the door. We're at the dock...you're safe...we made it."

"Praise Jesus!" she wailed, and they all started shouting and hugging each other, certain they had just survived a maritime disaster rivaling the sinking of the Titanic.

I was speechless. I just stood there looking on in amazement as they peeled off the life jackets and trooped off the boat with relief, their prayers obviously answered.

Bless their hearts.

6

Danger, for Real

The thing to remember when working on any boat or ship is that it's dangerous. That's capital-D, DANGEROUS.

First off, ships are made of steel, and steel hurts when you fall on it, smack your knee on it, or hit your head on it. When steel falls on you, it wins. Winches are more powerful than you are, and if you get a finger caught, in the future you will only be able to count to nine, or maybe eight. *So put your cell phone away and pay attention, Sparky.* Every boat I ever worked on had at least one guy nicknamed "Stubs or "Stubby."

One captain I sailed with didn't suffer fools gladly and he hated whiners. He most definitely ran the ship. After someone lost a finger in a deck winch, I overhead him say to the guy, "Here's the deal kid, ya gotta pay if ya wanna play. Jesus Christ, don't cry about a coupla' fingers. God gave ya 10 but ya only need a thumb and a pincher to get by, so ya got 8 spares. Shut the fuck up and get me a coffee."

Man, I loved that guy. He taught me a ton about sailing. But political correctness? Not so much. And whining? Never.

Things on a boat can go straight to rat shit in the blink of an eye. But that's the fun of it! Every day is a roll of the dice.

I saw a lot of mechanical damage over the years and quite a bit of human carnage. I myself have plates and screws in both wrists, two titanium knees and enough stitches to make a tent.

Here are a few pictures of bad days on the water:

Around midnight on a Friday night in October 1980, as guests aboard the Dutch cruise ship *Prinsendam* were winding down their evenings, a fire started in the ship's engine room. Most passengers, largely senior citizens, had eaten little for dinner due to rough seas. They were cruising 200 miles from Sitka and the winds were high. A voice over the stateroom speakers ordered everyone to the main lounge to wait until the "minor fire, now under control," could be handled and the smoke cleared from the rooms.

Given the seemingly tame nature of the situation, they arrived in all manner of dress and undress, from tuxedos and ball gowns to pajamas. But hours later, as the emergency worsened, drapes from the dining were taken down to be used as blankets, and the gift shop was raided for sweaters and warm clothing. After a harsh, stormy evening, the sea was now a dead calm as all passengers were ordered into the lifeboats.

Four Coast Guard, one Air Force and two Canadian helicopters were scrambled to pluck the 500 shipwreck survivors from crowded lifeboats in the cold Gulf of Alaska. Many were lifted in rescue baskets and carried to nearby ships, including a commercial tanker. But one lifeboat was missing.

I was quartermaster-of-the-watch aboard the Coast Guard cutter *Woodrush* (WLB-407), where we conducted an expanding square search pattern while continually scanning with radar and our eyes for the missing people. After six hours of searching, one of our lookouts spotted a dim light in the distance. We notified the other searching unit and the lifeboat was located. The remaining twenty survivors were rescued 20 hours after they had abandoned the burning cruise ship.

Thankfully, no lives were lost that night. *Prinsendam* sank seven days later.

**The Holland American cruise liner *Prinsendam* disaster
turned out to be the greatest rescue in Coast Guard history,
as not one life was lost.**

**A tug called the *Tioga* caught fire when
a 25-cent gasket gave out.**

The tug *Tioga* out of Sitka, Alaska was heading into town pulling a raft of logs to the pulp mill. It was just a beautiful boat, fresh out of the yard after a $100,000 re-fit. Unfortunately, a 25-cent gasket blew, allowing fuel to spray on a hot engine manifold. This is the result.

The crew of the Coast Guard cutter *Woodrush* fought the fire. Our guys were on board until the deck began to melt. The tug burned to the hull, and the charred remains can be seen to this day at the end of Olga Strait.

Crew members off the *Woodrush* fight the fire.

A two-ton lifeboat, twisted like a pretzel.
The sounds it made were unforgettable.

Here we have what remains of a lifeboat on a Great Lakes freighter after a loose cover got caught on the dock. It pulled the boat out of its cradle and jammed it against the dock as the boat moved forward. You just can't stop that much inertia.

7

Fast Eddie

Fans of the boats on the Great Lakes are lovingly referred to as "Boat-nerds." In fact, there is a not-for-profit website for Boatnerds that shares information about the various vessels on the Lakes. Their headquarters in Port Huron, Michigan overlooks the confluence of the St Claire and Black Rivers, and their website—www.boatnerd.com—receives over 20 million page views a month.

An all-time favorite of this crowd is the *Edward L. Ryerson*, which is definitely a special ship. She was built in 1960 in the traditional pilothouse-forward style. She was also built in an unheard of Art Deco style. Her owners spared no expense and to this day she is the holy grail for Boatnerds. She is a gorgeous vessel.

Photo courtesy of Roger LeLievre.

The *Edward L. Ryerson* is also known as "Fast Eddie," or simply the Queen of the Lakes!

She was laid up and out of service for years, but in 2006 the demand for steel brought her out of slumber and got her running again, much to the orgasmic delight of the Boatnerds. I was her second mate and relief first mate. In addition, due to the fact that I could actually spell and use words to form sentences, I was also designated public relations mate. No boat I had ever worked on before or since ever even had such a position.

A view from the bridge of the *Ryerson*.

From 2006-2009, as she traveled around the Great Lakes, adoring fans lined the shore, with kids pumping their fists in the air and people holding up signs that read "Salute!" The captain was always happy to accommodate, typically sending out the much-loved Great Lakes Master's Salute—long long long short short—in the ship's distinctive, throaty whistle. One time, the Canadian authorities responded thinking surely, with so many whistles, the ship must be in distress.

We got a *ton* of fan mail: letters, pictures, invitations to parties. I had hats made up and we sold hundreds in just a couple seasons. In fact, that's how Lisa—a bona fide Boatnerd—came into my life. But that's another story.

We sold these hats by the boatload.

Anyway, this guy, Larry Leverentz, sends us this picture he drew himself. At first we thought it was strange. Then we started to stare at it. Then we started to like it. Then we had the original framed and hung in the wheelhouse. We still have no idea where his mind was going, but we thought it was cool.

This original artwork, created for the crew of the *Ryerson*, reflects the reality that Boatnerds can be pretty nuts.

8

For Better or Worst

Mackinac Island, Michigan is one of the most beautiful places on this planet. It's very romantic as well, with the sound of vehicle traffic replaced by the calming clip-clop of horse's hooves. In the spring, lilacs abound and the air is heavy with their perfume.

It's no wonder Mackinac Island is a popular wedding destination. Often wedding parties would charter a ferry boat to host the reception, cruising slowly through the Straits of Mackinac. The sun setting behind the majestic towers of the Mackinac Bridge made for some spectacular photo opportunities.

That all makes for wonderful brochures, and many future brides fantasize about a gorgeous shipboard experience for their big day. For a few, "fantasy" is the key word. As captain of Arnold Line's 600-passenger M/V *Chippewa*, I ran many of these reception cruises. They were not all dream trips.

The *Chippewa* ferrying passengers to Mackinac Island.

The boss, Bruce, called me into the office on the Island to give me the particulars of an upcoming charter. There were to be approximately 50 guests, a small band and an open bar. The father of the bride was sparing no expense to make his little princess happy on her wedding day. He had already paid for a two-hour cruise, with the option to extend it if he wanted. Bruce said it was $400 an hour and the guy would pay me in cash as we went along, and to go ahead and take it.

OK, sounds pretty straightforward. Should be no problem. Optimism is a wonderful thing.

We finish the last run of the day and pull into the Island for the cruise. A group of bridesmaids jump on the boat and begin decorating. The band was setting up and the bartender was pouring drinks. Guests started trickling aboard, very loud and enthusiastic. Most obviously had a good head start on the party before coming down to us. *Hey, no problem, it's a festive occasion.*

The rest of the wedding party arrives to much cheering and fanfare, and we cast off. We motored slowly out of the harbor to the strains of the band playing the theme song from Gilligan's Island. *I hope I don't end up stranded on an island with this bunch.*

The door to the wheelhouse flies open and the maid of honor rushes in. Seems there's already a crises and we haven't even cleared the break wall yet. Hope it's not an omen.

"OMG," she slurs. ("Oh My God" in drunken sorority-speak.) "The bride forgot the special negligee she bought for the wedding night OMG!" It was still in the car back in Mackinaw City. "Like, OMG you have to get it. You just have to OMG." She's already drunk and getting teary.

"OK, relax," I tell her. "We're a full-service operation. Let's see what we can do." I called over to the Mac City dock and luckily the couple had valeted their car so dock had the keys. I got the description and where in the vehicle the conjugal bait could be found. Half hour passes and the word comes back that they have the package. The guys gave the box to the crew of the Island Express, the catamaran preparing to depart for the Island. Of course, the cat crew is having a ball making a few comments on the radio. I can't blame them. I would have done the same. I was just glad they found it. The M.O.H.'s sobbing entreaties were wearing me out.

By now we're well out in the Straits and the party is going full blast. For 50 people, they were making a lot of noise. Sounded like they were really tearing it up down below.

I stop the boat and wait for the cat. It soon appears, idling slowly alongside. The cat's purser, the Cuban, is on the bow with a box. As they drift past, he tosses it through the door to Jerry, my deckhand. He rushes it to the wheelhouse where the maid of honor wants to kiss us all. She was *not* a good-looking woman, plus she was blitzed.

"Sorry lady, party's out there," I said, gently pushing her out the door. "We'll keep the box in here until we get back." We throttle up and head for the bridge to the sounds of music, laughter, singing and the breaking of glass. Must be a good party.

The next emergency wasn't long in coming. Grandma, gassed up and showing the kids how to do the Watusi, falls down and cuts her finger on a broken wine glass. I patch Grandma up with a couple band-aids from the first aid kit and ease her out the door.

Now we're two hours into the cruise and I'm thinking we can wrap this up. The bartender just came up and reported—incredulously—that we were totally out of booze. These guys had sucked down every drop we had on board. It sounded like it. Well, that's that then. Party's definitely over.

Not so fast there, Cap.

Father of the bride stumbles in the door waving a fistful of hundreds. "'Nother hour, but we need more beer." Well, Bruce told me this might happen and we were fairly close to town, so in we go. A couple groomsmen wobble off down the dock, returning way quicker than I expected pulling a luggage cart heaped with more alcohol. Off we go again, but I'm a little worried now. This may be getting out of hand.

Daddy drops another $400 on me because the dock delay shortened the trip. *Man, I'm never getting home tonight.*

The band bailed as soon as we touched the dock for the resupply. So there was no music now, just loud off-key singing, screams and belligerent yelling. The bartender gave up and was in the wheelhouse with me. I kept the crew in there as well. It was just too crazy down below for sober people. When Daddy came staggering to the wheelhouse wanting still another hour (that would make it 5), I told him we were out of fuel and had to call it a night. Another hour and we would have been fishing drunks out of the lake for sure.

We couldn't get back to the dock fast enough. I was just glad we were dropping this load off on the Island so there was no chance of anybody driving. The crew put the ramp out and I went down to supervise the departure. The lower deck was a shambles. Empty beer cans, pizza boxes and garbage was everywhere. Puddles of vomit steamed on the deck. I could see blood from granny's fall. I was afraid to even look in the bathrooms. It smelled terrible.

Everybody was hammered: wedding party, guests, grandparents, even the kids. People were actually crawling off the boat on hands and knees. They had enjoyed 4 hours with nothing to do but drink, and they took advantage of every minute.

The bride and groom were screaming at each other and cursing a blue streak. Sobbing, the bride disappeared into the night with her bridesmaids, leaving the groom passed out on some hay bales on the end of the dock. The negligee was still in the box upstairs. As Daddy tottered down the ramp, he pressed a hundred dollar bill in my hand.

"For the crew," he mumbled. That was cool.

"Thanks, Dad." We called it a night.

The following morning on our first scheduled run of the day, we got to the Island just after 9:00 a.m. Unbelievably, the groom was still out cold on the hay, snoring, his face crusted with puke. That would have been a nice addition to the wedding album.

On the next trip, the bride is waiting on the dock. She won't even go look for her new husband. She asks me if I've seen the best man.

"No I haven't. Why?" Seems he was collecting and holding all the wedding envelopes, and judging from the tone of this crowd there was a ton of cash in them. He was missing in action and so was the money. He was last seen after the party disappearing down the street with a sketchy woman the dock porters described as a "skanky coke whore."

The bride came down looking for him for a week but he never showed up. She about had a stroke when I pointed out there were two other ferry lines he might have used to get off the island.

"By the way," I say. "You want your nightie? We have it in the wheelhouse."

"Keep it," she spat. "I never want to see it again." *OoooKay then.*

"Well, anyway, congratulations on your wedding."

She glares at me through bloodshot eyes. "Screw you, Captain."

Ouch. *Like, OMG.*

Captain of an Arnold Line ferry, 1994.

A few years down the road, I've moved on from Arnold Line and am working full-time on the ore boats. I'm home on vacation and get a call from Mike at Arnold Line asking if I would be available to do a wedding charter. It's been awhile, but why not. *OK.*

I'm back on my old girl, the *Chippewa*, steaming out to the Bridge with a couple of newlyweds and their guests. Beautiful evening. Calm seas. What could go wrong?

This was kind of a weird bunch. I sensed a lot of stress between some of the family members. Specifically, between the bride and a sister, June. June kept butting into everything and wanted to make the day about her. The bride was getting pissed off.

June had a little boy with her, about four or five years old. He was spoiled rotten and not in a good way. She barged into the wheelhouse and insisted I let Tommy steer the boat. He was a demanding, whiny little bastard, doughy and shaped like a loaf of bread. Mother just pampered him every second and expected everyone else to do the same.

She said to me, "Tommy wants to ride in here. He can sit on that bench and I'll check on him later." She had a fit when I told her that wasn't happening.

"We bought this boat for two hours. He can sit wherever he wants!"

"Guess again, lady," I calmly reply. 'I'm not your babysitter."

Snarling about having my job, she stormed out. I think, *Big deal, take it.* I'm just a relief guy anyway.

Roaming the boat under a black cloud, she was bitching about everything to anybody she could corner. She was putting a damper on the whole show.

After a while, little Tommy decided he didn't want to walk around anymore and begged his mom to carry him. The kid probably weighed 45 pounds. June must have been used to it because she scooped him up in her arms and staggered around holding him like an infant. I expected her to start breastfeeding him.

Coming up the forward stairs there were metal shutters that folded open. Because she was carrying Tommy crossways, when she went around the stairs she bounced his head off the corner of one of the shutters. Tommy immediately started screaming like he was being murdered, and bleeding like a stuck pig. Blood was gushing out of a pretty decent gash in his bean.

This brought the festivities to a screeching halt. Everybody's looking around, Tommy's going nuts, and June's shrieking she's going to sue the world. We get a pressure dressing on Tommy's noggin and I get on the radio. Tommy's really OK, just a cut on the scalp, but June wants a Coast Guard medevac. I tell her to calm down. We can get to the dock before the Coast Guard could even get going. Heading for the barn I can already see the flashing lights of the ambulance coming down the dock. An ambulance. *Jesus.*

The bride is livid. They're trying to get some wedding photos on the bow with the Mackinac Bridge in the background but the bow area is covered in blood. We didn't have time to rinse it all off. The photographer had to cut their feet off at the ankles to avoid showing blood in the pictures, since the bride's shoes were all bloody from accidentally stepping in a puddle of it.

I'm trying to organize things on the radio and since all the other boats can hear what's going on, I'm getting yucks and abuse from my fellow captains.

"Welcome back!"

"Bet you missed this!"

"Are you having fun yet?" *Oh, hell yeah.* I can't wait to get back to loading taconite.

We get to the dock and June is yelling and screaming so loud the paramedics at first thought she was the victim. They grab Tommy and shove him in the ambulance with June draped dramatically over his body. As they pulled away, she was wailing louder than the siren.

I turn to the bride and say, "Hey, we can go back out if you want to." She just looks at me, hikes up her dress and stomps off the boat in her bloody pumps, leaving footprints down the ramp.

The crew and I hose off the deck and then jump on the leftover beer. Someone might as well have a fun night.

I hope Tommy survived OK.

9

More Ferry Tales

Often, while loading taconite pellets and suffering an arctic blizzard in Duluth, or when loading coal in Ashtabula, Ohio and breathing coal dust instead of air, the ore freighter crews would be miserable. There had to be something better than this.

The common fantasy was to work on a nice clean cruise ship or ferry boat. How great would it be to load a cargo that walked aboard under their own steam? The reality, as any mariner with this experience knows, is that humans are the most dangerous and volatile cargo a ship can carry.

On the Alaska State Ferry M/V *Columbia* (the "Big C"), every Friday night in Seattle brought another 1000 passengers trooping aboard for the three-day run up to Skagway. The crew would be busy loading the car deck so paying little attention to the embarking travelers. Departing at 7:00 p.m. sharp, the *Columbia* motored her way out of Elliott Bay and headed, as Johnny Horton sang, "North to Alaska."

Photo courtesy of Alaska Marine Highway System

M/V *Columbia* runs along the Alaskan Marine Highway.

Now it's midnight, five hours later. The crew refers to the first hours of the trip as "shaking the tree to see what kind of nuts fall out." In a load of 1000 persons, odds were good there would be at least one total lunatic and sometimes more. Five hours on a boat would give them time to either get drunk or have their meds wear off and their "crazy-face" would appear.

Usually they could be discovered either screaming in the bar or barnstorming around the ship after the bar closed, causing chaos. Some were violent, some were drunk, and some were just nuts. No matter the mental malady du jour, the reality was, we were all stuck on a floating steel island with no law enforcement support. Whatever came up, the crew had to handle it: fire, floods and fights.

During the night, there would be five deck crew on watch— a mate, three deckhands and a fire watch—each working six hours on and six hours off. The deckhands worked a rotation: one hour on the wheel, one hour as lookout and one hour as rover, roaming around the ship keeping an eye open for weirdness. Most often the rover or the watchman would be the first one to discover trouble or have it reported to him.

Sometimes he could handle the situation himself, simply warning the knuckleheads to knock it off and go to bed. The real crazies didn't pay any attention though. At that point, the rover called the bridge, and the lookout and the watchman headed down to assist, calling the chief mate along the way.

The ship had an Emergency Response Team, or ERT, that responded to serious situations. Made up of the biggest or most experienced crew members, the ERT was an effective force. On a passenger ship, trouble had to be put down fast and as hard as necessary. The inmates after all, outnumbered the staff. On the Alaskan run, we got a lot of practice.

I was off watch and fast asleep when Gary threw open my door, yelled "ERT," and kept going. I threw on my clothes and tore topside to find agitated and frightened passengers clustered around the purser's counter. Seems there was some jackass running loose, threatening innocent people with violence and generally terrorizing the ship. The chief mate shows up and we head off to find this guy. As we go, passengers are pointing us in the right direction. He wasn't hard to follow.

We catch up to him aft on the fantail. He was climbing halfway up the deck rails and howling at the moon like a berserk werewolf. He was a pretty big boy and, in our experience, druggies and crazies have superhuman strength. We needed to take this guy down quick.

The chief mate said to me, "I'll get his attention, you grab him." *Good plan, let's do it!* Chief steps up to the rail and the guy swivels his head to look at him. I jump him from behind and wrap my arms around him, keeping his arms pinned, and take him down to the deck. I knocked the breath right out of him in the drop, which helped a lot.

Chief slaps the cuffs on him and we drag him off the deck into a vacant stateroom where we lock him to the bunk. I'm really glad there were no cell phone cameras as it was a hard takedown.

When we had a passenger in custody, there had to be a crewmember and a radio with him or her constantly. (With a woman, we also had a female crewman standing by.) Usually ERT members would split up the duty. It could be obnoxious to sit there for hours listening to some idiot scream curses and threats at you. That never bothered me though. At times it was actually pretty entertaining.

Our werewolf told me, "You have the upper hand now my friend…but it won't always be this way. I'm going to kill you, your family and your dog…I'm going to dig your grandparents up and kill them again." *Ooookay then.* Then he asked me for my name. *How dumb does this moron think I am?* I love my family and my dog and really don't want my grandparent's eternal slumber disturbed.

At that time, Alaska's governor's name was Sheffield, and he was always trying to bust our Union. So I tell the werewolf, "My name is Bill Sheffield and I live in Juneau. Good luck finding me, asshole." I keyed the radio first so the bridge crew could hear the conversation. They were all cracking up. We hated Sheffield. Might as well send a crazed stalker his way. Seemed like a good test for his security team.

Another trip, a huge logger came aboard. Nothing but a lump of solid muscle after three months of running choker cables up and down steep mountainsides. Most logging camps were dry, so this was the first alcohol this guy had imbibed all summer. He was so happy to be out of the woods he way overindulged and it hit him hard.

He was charging around the ship blackout drunk. He couldn't even talk, but was still wreaking general havoc. We cornered him on the top deck, the Solarium Deck, where the tent and sleeping bag crowd hung out. I jump on him and here we go…it's all I can do to hang on as he thrashed and whipped around.

We aren't trying to fight him, just subdue him. Now I know what it's like to ride a bull. After lasting the full eight seconds and deserving of a rodeo belt buckle, I got him down (I think he tripped) and was on top of him. I told the mate, "Quick, gimme the cuffs."

The Mate looks at me, pats his pocket, says, "Oops, I forgot 'em. Will be right back." *Seriously?* This guy's gonna get up and kill me in the meantime and he won't even remember it in the morning. Thankfully, I think he just decided it was time to sleep and was comfy on the nice steel deck, so I was able to keep him down until the mate got back with the cuffs.

**The Solarium Deck on M/V *Columbia*,
a.k.a. "Hippie Heaven" or the "Sty in the Sky."**

I ended up sitting with him most of the night while he slept it off locked to a bunk. He was an OK guy when he sobered up. We compared bruises and had some laughs about the night's adventures.

On another occasion, there was a mate named Ray that the crew absolutely hated. He was an arrogant, elitist asshat, always screwing with us and giving unnecessary—and often wrong—orders, just to be bossing someone. I got an ERT call that a drunk was beating on Ray topside. I ran up the stairs heading for the bar where I could hear screams and a lot of commotion.

I come flying around the corner, ready to jump in, but the bos'n stops me with an arm out: "Stand fast a minute, Lonnie. The guy's kickin' Ray's ass pretty good. Let's let him get a couple more shots in." One Mississippi two Mississippi three Mississippi, "OK, let's go." We peeled the guy off Ray and had another night babysitting in lockdown.

This time the crew was bringing the guy burgers, sodas and all kinds of goodies. Everybody was wanting to shake the hand that wasn't locked, and thank him. The guy was totally confused to find himself a hero. He thought he was going to jail. Arrangements had been made to give him to the state troopers in Petersburg, but we gave him a bag of food and snuck him off the boat in the baggage cart instead.

We often had groups of bikers on board. Alaska was known for some great rides. To forestall trouble, I made it a habit to find the biggest one, or whoever I thought was their leader, and approach him as soon as the trip started (and before the serious drinking started). I pointed out there was only one way off the ship and nowhere to hide or run away. If there was *any* trouble, they would be met at the first dock by the troopers and their Alaska trip would be over before it began. I said it in a conspiratorial tone like I was doing a favor for a bro and telling him a secret. I also lied and told them there was a law in Alaska that if one biker in the gang got arrested, the whole gang had to get off the ferry and all their bikes would be confiscated.

More often than not it worked. One time it didn't.

The leader of the pack himself was the doofus that went off the rails. Gooned out on whiskey, he started ripping the bar up when they cut him off. We got him down and cuffed with the usual wrestling. His buds must have believed me about the confiscated bikes because they helped us. He was locked to a post on the car deck because there were no empty staterooms and then, yup, I'm babysitting again.

The guy eventually calmed down, and although he was still drunk, he was cheerful about it. I'm shootin' the shit with him to pass the time and he's telling me some great stories. At one point, he goes, "You wanna see some pictures?"

Part of me wanted to say, "God, no," expecting shots of some horrible biker massacre. But I was bored and it was 3:00 a.m., so what the hell. "Sure, Dave," I said. (We were pals by now.) "Whatcha got?"

He reached into the pocket of his colors with his free hand and brought out a pile of grimy well-thumbed photos. "Check these out," he slurred proudly. "That's my old lady." Flipping through the stack I was treated to pictures of a husky middle-aged woman, stark naked and draped over a motorcycle in a variety of seductive poses. In a few pictures she was wearing bits and pieces of leather gear that didn't cover nearly enough to stop my eyes from bleeding.

"Wow, Dave," I managed to sputter out. "You're a lucky guy, thanks for sharing."

Dave came back to the ship a couple trips later, all cleaned up and sober as a judge. He just wanted to find me and thank me for what he called the "funnest night of my trip."

"OK, Dave. You are welcome...my best to the missus..."

Crossing the Gulf on the *Tustumena* in decent weather, we were running on a big ocean swell we called a lump. The ship was cruising easy when a passenger ran into the wheelhouse out of breath.

"We were eating in the dining room and a naked hippie flew by the window into the water." We hit the alarms…NOW THIS IS NOT A DRILL…man overboard, starboard side. The helmsman throws the wheel hard to starboard to swing the prop clear and begin a "Williamson turn" to bring the ship around and back down her previous track.

We can see the guy still afloat and splashing around. Even though its summer, the water temperature is about 48 degrees. Nobody can last long in that, especially naked. And he is naked. There was a neatly folded pile of clothes by the rail where he went over.

The only way to rescue the guy is to use the ship's lifeboat. This is not a sleek craft with a motor, but a clumsy heavy boat manned by four men, each pulling a 12-foot oar. There's a mate in the stern to steer and a guy in the bow as "hook man" responsible for releasing and re-hooking the lifting gear. The boat is launched pretty quickly. This is a sharp crew.

Off we go about 50 yards to reach the guy. As we get close, he starts swimming away. We chase him as fast as four men can row a big slow tub, but again he swims away, only slower this time. He's turning blue and its obvious he doesn't have much time left. Mate yells to the bow man, "bonk him with an oar." So we get closer and the bow man takes one of the 12-foot oars and, as gently as he can, whacks the idiot on the noggin'.

The swimmer's eyes rolled up and he stopped struggling. We grabbed him fast before he went under, and dragged him into the boat. He was as blue as a Smurf as we rowed back to the ship. The deck is now lined with passengers watching the show. *This is better than the travelogue showing in the lounge!* Again, I'm glad there were no cell phones to film us bapping him with the oar.

We get him aboard and treated for hypothermia. Later, with one of his hands cuffed to a bunk, I'm babysitting yet again. There's no jolly conversation with this flake, but I gotta ask him why he jumped.

"He told me to walk to town," he said.

"Who told you"?

"God told me."

"OK, as long as you had a good reason. But why no clothes?" I asked.

"I wanted to walk faster," he said. *Why didn't I think of that.*

I did hope we weren't in cosmic jeopardy for interfering with an order from

God, but the state frowned on us losing passengers. Too much paperwork.

So I'm sitting there reading a book and keeping one eye on him, when he starts to giggle. I key the radio because the bridge crew always likes to listen in. He's quiet for a while, then starts to giggle again. After the third time, I ask him, "What's so funny?"

More giggling and then he says, "I'm playing with my ass and you can't stop me." *Hooboy. That's a new one.* I shrug, "Hey, it's your keister, Brother. Have at it." I go back to my book.

M/V *Tustumena* crossing Kachemak Bay, Alaska.

I really don't care what he does. Whatever keeps him occupied until we can give him to the troopers works for me. But the bridge crew is just dying now. I'm having trouble keeping a straight face myself, thinking, *I'm glad I keyed the radio, otherwise nobody would believe me.*

We get out to Dutch Harbor and turn our disciple and his chapped ass over to the troopers and paramedic. He's still babbling about God and walking to town.

For the rest of the summer, if you addressed a member of the *Tusty* crew, "Good morning/afternoon, how ya doin'?" the response would be, "I'm playing with my ass and you can't stop me."

And the comeback was always, "Have at it, Brother."

10

Diplomacy on the High Seas
(or The Vodka Chronicles)

"In 1976 the Fisheries Conservation and Management Act established a 200-mile economic zone quadrupling the offshore fishing area controlled by the United States. The Coast Guard was responsible for enforcing this law."
—www.history.uscg.mil

In Alaska, the Fisheries Conservation and Management Act covered one hell of a lot of ocean: North Pacific, Gulf of Alaska and the Bering Sea. The big Coast Guard cutters (378s) began coming north out of San Francisco, Seattle and Hawaii, running what were called Alaska Patrols, or ALPATS. They were patrolling the waters north and west of Kodiak Island and then all the way out the Aleutian chain of islands to the Bering Sea.

The *Clover* on patrol in the Aleutians out of Dutch Harbor.

In 1977, I was a quartermaster on the Coast Guard cutter *Clover* (WLB-292), a black-hulled work boat based in Sitka, Alaska. Unlike the 378s, we were already "up north." The crew was beyond excited when word came down from

District that *Clover* was to embark on an Alaska Patrol herself. This was mainly to be seen and "show the flag," but also to board and visually confirm the foreign fleets' adherence to the new law.

Even though the United States claimed water out to the 200 mile limit, foreign fishing boats were allowed to come in and fish species Americans, at the time, considered trash fish. Alaska pollock, Atka mackerel and grey cod were fish the Russian, Japanese and Korean boats were licensed to harvest. They were forbidden to catch salmon, halibut or crab. To be caught doing so could result in the seizure of the vessel and huge fines to the sponsoring government. Our job was to oversee these regulations and keep everybody honest. Easier said than done.

The crew was eager to go "out the chain" and see some new country. From other Coasties, we had all heard stories about "the chain." Barren windswept mountains and active volcanoes. There were no trees due to the constant and vicious wind. The Navy base out on Adak Island had a scrawny pine tree with a white picket fence around it and a sign that read "Adak National Forest." That explained another Aleutian saying: "There's a woman behind every tree."

Locals also knew there was only one daily weather report out the chain: "It's ugly and it's gonna get uglier." Right on both counts.

Picnic weather out the chain.

Clover's first stop was Coast Guard Base Kodiak. The officers (the Os) were scheduled for a series of briefings on ALPAT policy and what to expect. Meanwhile the crew headed to the enlisted club, the Golden Anchor, to down as many beers as possible before we left. We had a great time, culminating in a brawl with some guys from the base.

Radiomen were required to send and receive messages in Morse code, and experienced operators could recognize individuals by their sending technique, or "fist." The biggest insult a radioman (RM) could give another was to call him a "lid" or a "shit-fist." Our radioman was labeled a "shit-fist" by a local RM and the fight was on. It was mainly a lot of wrestling around, wild punches, and overturned tables. Since we were the visitors, we got kicked out, returning to the ship tattered and laughing. This ALPAT stuff was a blast so far.

Once underway, we headed around the north end of Kodiak Island, through the tide rips in Ouzinkee Narrows and then into Shelikof Strait. The strait was open-ended to the west and therefore the welcome mat to the Aleutian weather. It got snotty right away and guys began regretting their hangovers.

There was a gaggle of Japanese trawlers working out of a bay near Chignik and the captain had a plan. The crew rigged some new lights on the mast so in the dark the *Clover* would appear to be just another fishing boat. Since we were new in the area and hadn't been spotted yet, the idea was to cruise into the middle of the Jap fleet like a Trojan horse and surprise them all.

We waited until dark, pulled out of the bay we were hiding in, and headed for the Jap fleet. We could see their lights and as we got closer it appeared our plan was working. Suddenly the radio crackled to life. Since they were so close it boomed in: HAHAHAHAHA FUK YOUUU, AMELICAN CO-SCOD... FUK YOUUUU...HAHAHAHA.

Cap shrugs, "Aw dammit, well, go ahead and light us up." All our searchlights come on and we start cruising slowly through the fleet, blasting them with a million candlepower, and logging names and vessel numbers. There must have been a dozen. Since they were not actively engaged in fishing, Cap decided not to actually board any. We called it a night and kept heading farther out the chain.

The next day, we sight some Russian factory trawlers actively fishing. Actually, you smell these boats long before you see them. Clouds of seabirds surround them and when you get close, the screeching of the birds drowns out the sound of the engines. These are large vessels, over three hundred feet long. They are engaged in pelagic trawling, towing huge nets until they fill, then winching them up a stern ramp onto the ship. When they empty the nets, the fish are dropped down to a factory line where they are processed. Some are frozen into fillets and the trashier fish are ground up into fishmeal, used for animal feed.

Cap says, "OK, were gonna check a few of these guys. Boarding parties meet in the wardroom." We gather into two five-man teams so we can do two ships at a time. That's actually pretty ambitious, as even though we can see several boats, they are scattered over several miles and none are close together.

My team is led by Ensign Brathwaite, who was an eager beaver and a first-rate dick. He was so excited to be going on a boarding he couldn't sit still. And he wanted, so bad, to go armed. He reminded me of Barney Fife. This was the '70s and we weren't trying to be a SWAT team, more like fisheries observers.

The captain didn't think weapons were necessary, but he finally told Brathwaite, "OK, take one .45 but keep it out of sight." I thought he should have given him one bullet to keep in his pocket. Besides, what the hell were five of us going to do with one pistol on a boat with over 200 Russians?

We hear BOARDING PARTY AWAY on the loudspeaker and off we go in a small inflatable Zodiac, getting delivered like a pizza. We get to the Russian boat and they drop a rope ladder over the side. There's a pretty big sea running and we're shooting up and down the side of this rusty barnacle-covered hull trying to grab the ladder. I was praying the inflatable didn't tear.

The catcher-boat unloading to the mothership.

We take turns waiting until we're at the top of a swell and jump for the rope. In wetsuits, climbing up this flimsy ladder, we pass some open portholes. Grinning faces of large Russian women appear, followed by beefy arms reaching out trying to squeeze our balls as we climb past. Jake's on the ladder above me twisting and shrieking like a little girl. I thought, *Jesus, if he lets go, we're all dead.* The ladies were just having fun with us though, and they allowed us to finish our climb without further violation.

Man, did this ship ever *stink!* Fish guts, dead fish, slime, and a couple hundred sweaty Russian bodies put up quite a cloud. They were just finishing recovering a trawl. A huge net lay on the deck bulging and thrashing with thousands of fish. A crewman stepped forward and pulled a line called a "zipper" and it opened the trawl. Fish started pouring down a chute into the processing plant below deck.

As mentioned, they were not allowed to keep salmon, halibut or crab, so as one of those species flopped on deck it was tossed back down the long stern chute to go back into the ocean. Only thing was, waiting at the bottom of the chute was a "raft" of six or eight monstrous Stellar sea lions. Adults go anywhere up to 2400 pounds and these guys all looked like adults.

As a 100-pound halibut went skidding down the ramp, one of these creatures would rear up out of the water, grab the fish in the air and just devour it, ripping their head from side to side and disappearing momentarily in a cloud of blood and fish guts. The sheer power and the violence was stunning. There were no safety chains closing off the ramp and I shivered to think what might happen to a young Coastie, were he to "accidentally" fall down that chute. I doubted it would cause a nuclear response from Washington, so I stepped back from the edge.

It was time to get down to business. The first mate greeted us and took us into the wardroom (officer's dining room) to meet the captain. Some of these guys spoke English, but most did not. There were a lot of grins, head nodding and gestures. Their cap was a salty looking guy, maybe in his 50s, wearing a thick seaman's sweater and blue jeans. His English was halting but we could understand each other. In the corner stood an unsmiling man with a notebook. He was taking notes on everything we or the captain said. We learned he was the "political officer," or "party man," there to keep tabs on the crew and make sure they were thinking "correctly."

There are maybe a dozen of us around the table, five Coasties and the rest Russians. First thing, out comes the vodka. *Gotta drink a toast to the Coast Guard!* I look at Brathwaite and he nods. Roger that, orders are orders. Down the hatch then. But wait, now we have to drink a toast to Russia. Gulp, again. Down the hatch.

Ensign Brathwaite realizes that this could go on all day. He wants to regain control of the situation, although he never had it in the first place. He stands up suddenly, and out of his wetsuit pops the .45. Thud. It lands right smack in the middle of the table. You could have heard a pin drop. There are big eyes all around.

The political officer takes a step forward to see better. It's dead quiet, all eyes on the captain. Slowly he reaches out and picks up the gun. Turning it in his hand, he looks it over. I'm thinking, *Oh God, we're done for now. But I bet he shoots Brathwaite first, so if that's the last thing I see, that would at least be cool.* Finally the captain smiles, reverses his grip on the pistol and hands it back to Brathwaite. "Wery nice, but you not need here." So we're off to a great start.

Then the political officer drops a sheet of paper on the table. He wants us all to write down our names and home addresses. Sounds like bullshit to me, but Brathwaite is so embarrassed by the gun thing he can't grab the pencil fast enough. Passing the paper to me he says, "Do it."

Screw that. I don't want to be signed up for some Russian record of the month club or worse, on some sleeper cell hit list. I write: Harry Nutz, 6969 Dryhump Lane, Sheepdip, Montana, and pass the paper to Jake.

Jake's a dumbass. "That's not your name," he proclaims in a loud voice. Glaring at him I hiss, "It is today." Brathwaite gives me the stink eye, pissed that I'm not following his new best friend, the political officer's, orders. Too damn bad.

We divide up and start our inspections. Quartermaster was a navigation rate so I go to the bridge to check their catch logs and look at their charted fishing spots. They were using American charts but the logs were all in Russian. There was not a whole lot I could check, but this was more like show biz anyway. They didn't really know what I was looking for. I pretended to pour over the charts, clicking my tongue and shaking my head now and then. It really did appear these guys were following the rules, so after a half hour or so I nodded and told the first mate, "OK. All good here." I don't know, it probably was.

He grinned from ear to ear and out came the vodka. *Gotta toast the good fishing!* This was gonna be a long day. He got as chatty as he could with his limited English and proudly showed me pics of his family back in Russia. He told me he hadn't been home in a year and he missed his house. When their ship got full, a mothership came out from Russia, took their catch, gave them more food and fuel, and left them there to fish some more. They were just so thrilled to have some new company. We were like new neighbors down the block come to call. They couldn't offer enough hospitality. It was a little touching.

Alaska Coast Guard patrol, 1977.

He says the captain has lunch ready for us, so down to the wardroom we go. I'm still wearing my wetsuit, but they are two piece sets so I've unzipped the top and released the crotch piece, allowing it to dangle like a short rubber tail. As we walked down the passageway, giggling Russian women who should have had John Deere tattooed on their foreheads kept coming up behind me and grabbing my tail, pulling on it and laughing. Smiling himself, the mate kept yelling "Nyet Nyet," and shaking a finger at them with little result. I couldn't help grinning myself. This was a horny bunch.

We go into the wardroom and the captain's there with his personal steward-ess or *bufetchitsa*. She is one hot gal, with beautiful Slavic features and wearing a stylish red-and-white polka dotted dress. I later learn that Russian trawler cap-tains have no say over crew and officers assigned to his ship, but he is allowed to hire his own *bufetchitsa*. The captain sees me staring and gives me a wink. This guy's a player. I'm impressed.

The table's groaning under an incredible spread: black bread, a large selec-tion of meats and cheeses, jams, jellies, pastries, and of course vodka.

In pride of place, in the center of the table, was a silver tray heaped with fish eyeballs. No matter where you were in the room it seemed the tray followed you. They must have been raw and the Russians were popping them in their mouths like grapes. I couldn't do it. The captain laughed and nodded as he bit into another one. We had a fun meal with many toasts, and international rela-tions were going well.

At one point the political officer left the room for a few moments. The captain looked around carefully and leaned forward. "You, me, we seamen. Washington, Moscow, ehhhhhhhh," he said, making a gesture of two thumbs down. Then he sat back looking innocent as the party man returned. Cap gave me another wink.

That summed it all up for me and I never looked at those ragged, stinking trawlers the same way again. They were just guys like us, doing a job and missing their families. I felt a little sorry for them.

The capper of the whole day came as we prepared to depart. The Zodiac from *Clover* was standing by under the rope ladder. The seas had built during the day and it was going to be a tricky maneuver to get safely aboard. Ensign Brathwaite was fried, having had way too many vodka toasts, trying to make up for pulling a gun on the Russian captain. In order to get him back in our boat, the Russians slung a cargo net and put Brathwaite inside. Using their crane, they lowered him down to the waiting Zodiac.

I was laughing at him and so was my new buddy, the first mate. I don't think the Russians had a lot of respect for Brathwaite. Shaking my hand and giving me a hug, he waved as I grabbed the ladder and disappeared over the side. This time the ladies let me pass with no molestation, but they did wave and blow kisses from the open portholes.

"Za zdorovje!" they called. *For health!*

11

Greenhorn Blues

If we are lucky growing up—and I mean *really* lucky—someone will cross our path who will give us an incredible boost. This individual will guide us toward developing maturity and an awareness of the world beyond our puny, self-centered selves. For me, this person was able-bodied seaman John Bascombe, who was a United States Merchant Mariner.

The year was 1974 and I had just finished my third year of college at Michigan State. I had no real direction in life, was hating school, and my grades showed it. So far, college had pretty much been a waste of money. Well, except for the parties. Those parties were epic!

Growing up, I had always been fascinated by boats and ships. The lure of the sea had been planted in my brain early listening to my dad's stories about his Navy service on a submarine chaser in Hawaii during WW2. I got seaman's papers right out of high school, but so far had been unable to land a boat job. So I had basically gone to college as a fallback career option. Truth be told, my parents made me go, but my heart wasn't in it. *Did I mention there were parties?*

Then, in the summer of 1974, I caught a break. My dad got me an interview with the manager of U.S. Steel Great Lakes Fleet supply warehouse in Sault Ste. Marie, Michigan. The Soo, which is how the locals refer to the area, is on the St. Marys River and is home to a set of locks ships must transit to compensate for the different water levels between Lake Superior and Lake Huron.

My life finally got underway in 1974
when I landed a job on the *Olds*.

74

Making no promises, the manager took my information and that was that. I figured I was doomed to go back to school in the fall. To my surprise, I got a call in August that there was an opening for a porter—read: dishwasher, cabin steward and janitor—on the *Irving S. Olds*, a 625-foot iron ore carrier owned and operated by U.S. Steel. It was nothing more than an entry-level, foot-in-the-door job. Me: *Oh, hell yeah!*

I said goodbye to my girlfriend of three years, much to her distress and disappointment, and headed for the Soo to catch the boat. As a freighter came out of the lock downbound (heading down river), a small supply tug named the *Ojibway* went out from her dock below the locks, loaded with supplies and returning/new crewmembers. Pulling alongside the massive ship as it slowly rolled down the river, a crane swung pallet loads of groceries and gear over onto the hatch covers.

On the deck of the boat it was a well-choreographed ballet, even though to a "greenie" like me it looked like chaos. Twenty men wearing variously colored hardhats—to differentiate their jobs—swarmed on the pile of gear and rapidly started hauling it off in all directions. A cocky little guy in a white hard hat was overseeing the program and shouting orders and curses in equal measure. OK, maybe more curses. He really had everyone jumping. I soon discovered he was the chief (or first) mate, meaning he was the captain's second-in-command and the guy who ran everything concerning deck operations.

After the supplies were loaded, it was time for the crew change. Several men with sea bags were standing forlornly on the deck of the *Ojibway*, their vacations over. They were now staring at the prospect of another three months of lonely sailing up and down the Lakes. They were all shaking their heads and chuckling at my obvious—and horribly misplaced—excitement. On the ship, the departing crewmembers were fairly dancing in place, already tasting their first "freedom beer" at the Antlers bar, whose welcoming lights could be seen twinkling on the beach over the starboard rail.

I was the last one to throw my bag over onto the deck and step across onto the ship. Man, it was *big!* I was frozen in place, mouth agape, watching the hustle and bustle around me. The first mate suddenly appeared right in my face, eyes bugged out and veins popping in his neck, spraying spit all over me when he talked (yelled).

"Enjoying the view, pissant?" were the first words ever spoken (screamed) to (at) me on a ship in what would become my 40-some-year seagoing career. "How 'bout you quit pullin' your pud and help *move this gear!*"

It's hard to forget a nice welcome like that.

I frantically turned around to jump back to the safety of the *Ojibway*, but it had already cast off. As it headed back to shore, the off-going crewmembers clustered on her back deck laughing, waving, pointing, and flipping middle fingers at us, their unfortunate brothers who were still humping supplies as the *Olds* rumbled away down the river.

You bastards! They were strangers, but at that moment I hated every single one of them.

If she hadn't already pulled away, I would have jumped back on the *Ojibway* before she left.

I dropped my bag and started wildly grabbing boxes, any boxes. I had no clue where any of them were going but I was, by God, picking them up. I couldn't believe I left my smoking-hot girlfriend's warm bed for this.

A big guy in a yellow hard hat bumped me on the shoulder and said in a low, gravelly voice, "Here ya go kid, don't worry about that guy, give me a hand with this." I gratefully took an end of the box he was carrying and headed off up the deck, hopefully out of range of the obviously rabid first mate.

The guy said his name was John, and he was one of the AB's (able seaman). Moving up the deck, John told me it really wasn't that bad all the time, and that the mate, Leroy, was really a pretty good guy, normally. "He just tends to get a little excited when things are happening fast," he said. Actually, he told me with a deep chuckle, Leroy's greeting would be a story I would appreciate someday. He called it "vintage Leroy," and said the crew was already laughing about it and not to take it personally.

John also told me that many new guys actually *did* quickly climb back on the *Ojibway* after one of Leroy's greetings, and the fact I stayed and started picking up boxes was a big point in my favor. So three minutes aboard and I had already learned my first lesson: New guys are fair game. They want to see how you are going to fit in, and nothing like sudden stress and abuse to cut that discovery process short. *What a buncha dicks,* I thought. But I couldn't wait to be one too!

My learning curve was steep. I got no hand-holding and very little advice. *It's sink or swim, Princess.* The first night out, the deck crew had been working all day painting the deck around the bow. Being the porter, my room was aft, at the rear (stern) of the boat—on the Great Lakes, even 1000-foot long ships are called boats—so I wasn't aware of all this painting activity. Around midnight, we were still in the river and I went forward to rubberneck a bit. It was summer, so I went up on the bow in just shorts and no shoes. I watched us making the turn at Moon Island, walked around a bit, and then went back to bed. My feet were feeling kind of sticky but I wrote that off to the heat.

The next morning at breakfast, the bos'n was going nuts: "Some son-of-a-motherless whore walked barefoot all over my fresh bow paint job!" Apparently there were footprints everywhere so now he had to completely re-do the job. He wanted the captain to order the entire crew to muster barefoot so he could inspect the bottoms of everyone's feet.

The captain told him to settle down and have another donut. I pulled off my now-red-stained socks and threw them over the side, but it took weeks for that paint to wear off my feet.

The next day, one of the crew members told me the captain's private lounge was the crew rec room. So I go in, thinking, *Wow, this is sweet.* I kicked back in a big recliner, ate an apple from the fruit bowl on the table, and just made myself at home. I hung around for a while and left.

A bit later I was talking to one of the deckhands and said, "Hey, let's go up to the rec room."

"Whadya mean up? The rec room's down below."

"No, the nice one with the recliner and the big TV," I said.

"Jesus Christ, are you outta your mind? That's the captain's living room," he sputtered. "You get caught in there, they'll never find your body."

Man, I was so *easy*, so green…and so very lucky.

I eventually found my way, and after I came out on top in the popular "mail buoy watch" joke, John took me under his wing and started teaching me the craft of being an able seaman. He taught me how to coil and throw a heaving line with pinpoint accuracy, and how to run a deck winch. Just as importantly, he taught me the million little traditions a proper sailor needs to know on the Lakes. Like, never walk on the starboard side of the ship because that's the "captain's walk," and it must always be kept clear and clean.

But he was always holding out on showing me knotwork. And he was a master of the craft. Becket Bend, Carrick Bend, Bowline on a Bight, Spanish Bowline, long splice, short splice...John knew these like breathing air. His fancy knotwork was amazing. I was constantly ragging him—"show me show me"— and he would just laugh.

Then one day I said, "*Teach* me."

"OK," he said. "There's a big difference between 'show me' and 'teach me,' so yeah, I'll teach you." The only thing was, he said it would cost me $100 per knot to learn. "If you have skin in the game," he said, "you'll pay more attention."

He wasn't wrong, and I wasn't about to argue. I wanted to learn those knots, bad. I gave him $200 and he taught me the Monkey Fist and the Turk's Head. The Monkey Fist knot would usually be tied around a large ball bearing and then clipped to a light line called a "heaving line." This line, using the weighted Monkey Fist for distance, would be thrown to the dock and used to haul over the ship's heavy mooring lines.

A deckhand throws a Monkey Fist and a heaving line to the dock.

After a few weeks, when there wasn't a square inch of the ship without some form of these two knots lashed in various stages of competency—mostly bad—he gave in. With a smile, he taught me cox combing and grapevine seizing for free.

What I came to learn, over time, was that John had been a merchant seaman in WW2, and had been on a ship torpedoed on the run to Murmansk, Russia. He had floated for days, half-frozen in a lifeboat, only surviving by huddling under the corpses of his dead shipmates. He was very fortunate to still be alive and I was awed that he continued to sail. "It's what I do," was his answer to that unfathomable question.

He rarely talked about his ordeal, but one time when he and I were sitting out on deck tying knots and shooting the shit, I asked him why, after all his time at sea, he had never gone for a license and a captain's job of his own. For surely, the guy could do it all, so he was definitely qualified.

He looked off in the distance, spit some snus in a can, and told me: "When the torpedo hit, I was on the bridge. It was my shift on the wheel. The captain was an old Norwegian, strict as a schoolmaster but a total professional. We started going down by the stern...going down fast...musta taken the fish in the engine room.

"Cap was as calm as if he was in church. He turned to me and said, 'Off you go now John, you are relieved.' I said, 'But how about you, Cap, aren't you coming?' He calmly drew on his pipe and looked out the window, turned and said, 'John, I have men in the engine room that aren't getting out. I am their captain...how can I leave them? I will *not* leave them. But you go now. This is my load to carry.'"

John kind of choked up and said, "I ran then...I was afraid. I lived but he stayed. He stayed with his men and his ship. His last words were...'it's my load to carry.' Son, I don't know if I could have done that. So in answer to your question, my philosophy has always been: Don't lift the weight if you can't carry the load. I'm a good able seaman. I know I can carry *that* load, so that's enough for me."

Suddenly, my whining about my student loan debt seemed pretty damn insignificant.

As time went on, I practiced and practiced on my knots, and when I was done I would show them to John. But they were never quite right. He was always pointing out a tweak I should have made here or could have made there. He reminded me that knotwork on an item was to enhance that item, that the knotwork wasn't supposed to be the focal point. But when it did stand alone, he said, it should stand proud. Oh, and the ends should never, ever show!

**Grapevine seizing and three-strand Turk's Head on
a boat hook—with no ends visible!**

I knew I had arrived the day I showed him a Monkey Fist I'd tied that was tight as a banker's heart and pretty as a mermaid's smile. John looked at it from all angles, tossed it back to me and said with a grin, "Fine work, shipmate." No praise was ever more appreciated.

John has long since passed on to Fiddler's Green, but I still make certain every knot I tie would earn his high "fine work" stamp. *Thanks for everything, John. Fair winds and following seas, my friend.*

⚓

12

Fresh Fish and Sore Fingers

The Coast Guard ship I was stationed on was moored directly across the channel from the commercial harbor in Sitka, Alaska. While going about my daily duties I could watch dozens of fishing boats coming and going, and to me they looked romantic and cool.

In my off time I would walk the docks to get a closer look, and often get an invite to come aboard a vessel for a coffee or a cocktail in a snug wheelhouse or galley.

This went on for my four years of government servitude, and during that time I made many good friendships in the fishing fleet. When I got out of the Coast Guard in 1981, I was invited to join the four-man crew of the F/V *Donna Lee* for the spring halibut opening. Man, I was in heaven!

In reality, this wasn't as wonderful as it first sounds. There is much to do to get the boat ready and this is all unpaid labor. You are earning your spot on the crew. The fishing gear has to be organized and overhauled, the boat has to be provisioned and fueled up, and everything takes time and manpower. But if you expect to be on the crew, you are expected to be there doing the preliminary work.

I didn't have anything else going on that spring, and after four years in the Coast Guard and two years on iron ore freighters, a paint brush definitely fit my hand. So I volunteered to paint the boat. I spent two weeks on that project, and when I was done that old fishing boat just sparkled in the weak Alaskan sun. Or as my old Great Lakes bos'n used to put it, it shined up like "a diamond in a goat's ass." Whatever that meant.

Now we're going fishing for halibut on a two-week opening. We are going up north, out of Cross Sound, into the Gulf of Alaska, and out into what is called the Fairweather Grounds. This is a shallow shelf that extends out into the Gulf before dropping off to unimaginable depths. Since halibut are bottom feeders, we want to set our gear so it's not too deep but still on the bottom where there may be a lot of movement.

The Fairweather Grounds could be dicey though, because if the wind came up out of the west, the seas hitting the shallow shelf would build to giant size quickly and there was nowhere close by to hide. The weather report looked good so out we went.

The *Donna Lee* was what was called a "long-liner," meaning she set her gear on the bottom in a quarter mile long string. We strung a line, broke that off, marked it with a flag at each end, then went on to make another "set," and then another, until all her gear was out. By that time, the first set had "soaked" for several hours or so. Then the boat went back, hooked on to an end, and started to "haul gear."

The *Donna Lee* looked like romance and adventure all rolled into one.

The baited hooks were attached to the line with big steel clothespins, and as the line came up and re-wound on the drum, the winch operator unclipped them and hooked them on a rack. When a halibut came up, he used a bat to stun it and then threw it in a bin. It was up to the crew to process it: gut it, clean it and then drop it through a hatch into the ice hold. From there, another crewman would fill its belly with ice, then layer it into a bin and cover it with more ice.

It was a very efficient system but it never stopped, going day and night for two weeks. The crew was four men, so each worked 18 hours on deck with 6 hours to sleep. I have never fallen asleep so fast or slept so hard as during those brief sleep breaks.

When I woke up each day, my hands were clenched like claws and I could barely open them. As I went on deck to begin my 18-hour shift, the crew would have heated water in a teapot to pour on your hands to get them unclenched and useful again.

As the new guy—the greenhorn—I spent most of the haul in the ice hold. Using an ice scoop, I would have to move a hundred pounds of ice out of a bin to make room for the incoming fish. My hands got so sore I could hardly hold the scoop. Every couple minutes a huge, slimy 100-pound halibut would drop down on me, sometimes still twitching. I had to hurry to get it iced and stashed before the next one came bombing down. This was a long way from the romantic life I had envisioned as a fisherman!

We filled the boat and headed to shore. We were a long way from town but the fish company had stationed a buying scow in a bay up north by the Grounds. This was a large barge with a house on it, where boats could offload their catch and receive credit. Another large company boat would come out from town and move it all into the cannery.

The buying scow where we swapped fish for cash.

These scows wanted boats to sell to them so they offered many perks: hot showers, beer and even pot, if crew so desired. (*What can I say? This was the '80s.*) So we got offloaded and headed back out, possibly feeling a bit more mellow.

The worst deal for me happened on a day when we were almost full. There was not a lot of room left in the ice hold when we caught the biggest beast so far: A 9-foot long halibut weighing at least 350 pounds. But there was only about two and a half feet of clearance left in the ice hold when they dropped that monster down on me.

He was so big his tail was still sticking up on deck. I didn't know what I was gonna do with him! Finally I got him bent around and down into the hold, but the only way I way to get him up on the pile was for me to first lay up there and then pull him up on top of me. So there I was, flat on my back, pulling this creature up and over me, trying to slide him over my rain gear and up into position.

I get him right on top of me—so there's like zero clearance now—and he starts twitching and flopping. His nerves are still firing! *Fishy prick!* Now I'm trapped under him while he's bucking and vibrating, and I'm sure I'm probably going to die now too. But hey, I'm already iced down, so they can just take me straight into town, right where I am.

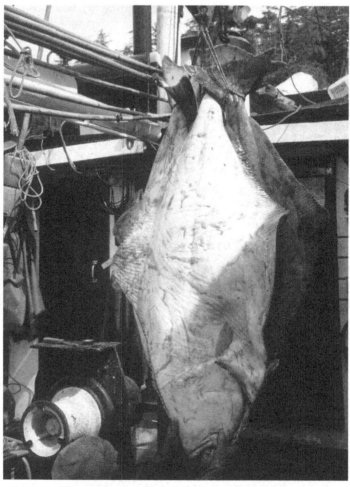

The fishy prick that about killed me.

I finally slid out from under this massive piece of sushi as he decides to lay still, with me totally covered head to toe in a thick coat of fish slime. I might even have peed a little.

When we got back to town, I just threw my clothes and rain gear in the garbage can at the head of the dock. Then I cashed my check and swore never again. *Screw this fishing crap.* I went back to the boats with the regular hours and overtime pay.

13

I Meet the Locals

The night was young and, like a mermaid's smile, full of promise. I was newly arrived in Sitka, Alaska, courtesy of the United States Coast Guard. After growing up in the small village of Pellston, Michigan, I thought Sitka would be pretty much the same. That was the first of my many erroneous preconceptions of life on the Last Frontier.

Thompson Harbor in Sitka, Alaska.

As with many Southeast Alaskan communities, the population of Sitka was almost evenly split between Caucasians—people of European ancestry—and Indigenous Indians from several Alaskan tribes: the Tlingkats, Aleuts, Haidas and Athabaskans. The latter were all referred to by the government as "Alaskan Natives" (capital N).

The tribes all co-existed in relative harmony but shared a bloody history of internecine hatred. Referring to a person of one tribe by the name of another would invite a scathing response, on a sliding scale of violence relative to the location, time of day, and their level of drunkenness.

The common denominator was a history of slavery, domination and out-right brutality laid on them by Russian overlords back when Alaska was first settled as a Russian colony. So the hatred of Russians was in their DNA, although an exception was made for a strange devotion to the Russian Orthodox Church. This hatred would manifest itself in slurred curses and physical assault in direct proportion to the amount of alcohol consumed on any given day or night. After enough "hooch," the label "Cossack" applied to all, and specifically to the nearest "Russian bastards."

Having just arrived to the region, I didn't yet know all this. But it was a lesson I was soon to learn.

Ship's liberty granted, I was sharing a table with my fellow Coasties at the Kiksadi Club, a rough-cut roadhouse on the edge of town. The place was called the "Kiksodomy" by the locals. With peanuts on the tables and sawdust on the floor—either to soak up spilled beer or shed blood from the many fights—it was a cozy place to unwind from the rigid daily routine of the Coast Guard.

One of my shipmates came running in, pointing out the door, and shouting, "Hey, there's a guy outside beating the shit out of some woman." The general response from my buddies was: "Big deal...so what...this is Sitka." But being fresh out of boot camp and brimming with righteous idealism, I wasn't standing for that. Jumping to my feet I said something heroic and stupid like, "Not on my watch," and tore out the door.

There in the gravel parking lot I saw a skinny "Native" man whaling away on a "Native" woman who must have gone 350 pounds, at least. He was shrieking what I assumed to be curses in some long forgotten dialect, as they both huffed around in circles like boxers.

I jumped in, grabbed the guy, and threw him to the ground. Turning to see if the woman was suitably grateful—and expecting thanks—I got hit in the chest by a human bulldozer. Swinging huge fists wildly and connecting with more than a few, she attacked me, screaming, "Cossack prick! You stop hurt my Johnny!"

What the...*I'm the good guy here!* A rolling boil with the locals would be a fine way to end the evening, but its barely six bells on the dog-watch—a.k.a. 7 p.m.—and my night's just getting started. It's way too early to get my ass kicked.

I covered my head, trying—and so far failing—to deflect her blows, when the guy gets up, jumps on me and *bites me* in the back of the neck. Now he has a death grip on my shoulders and a snaggly broken tooth sunk in deep, obviously blaming me for his lover's chronically unfaithful actions and/or some Russian stealing his great-great-great-grandfather's dog. These guys hold a grudge for centuries.

Thrashing around like a harpooned halibut, dodging her fists and trying to shake him off, I see her pick up an empty wine bottle and move in for the kill.

I frantically spun around and with a last gasp of effort, my neck-biting passenger swung out horizontally like an overloaded Maytag. As he flew around, his thrashing boot caught his enraged queen right between her bloodshot "runnin' lights" (eyes, in Coast Guard-speak) with a dull thud. Gurgling a sigh, she dropped like a stone.

Now sobbing with remorse, he peeled off my back and dropped to his knees beside his fallen sweetheart. Her huge mass barely twitched with the effort of smashing a ham-sized fist into his face. Howling like rabid animals, the circling crowd and the punching, kicking couple rolled back into the "Kik," leaving me standing there tattered and bloody on the gravel.

The chief bos'n came over and draped a beefy arm around my shoulder. "Welcome to Sitka, kid. This happens all the time. We like to let the new guys have a go, though. It's fun to watch. Forget it. Let's get a beer."

So much for smiling mermaids.

14

Mark's Refreshing Swim

There are no roads connecting the island communities of Southeast Alaska with the rest of the world. Everything that comes in to the island cities and villages of the Alexander Archipelago comes by air or sea. Alaska Airlines flies a daily "milk run" from Seattle. The big ferries of the Alaska Marine Highway System bring in semi-van loads of produce and hardware, as well as passengers and cars, but it's a drop in the bucket.

The vast majority of fuel and goods arrive from Seattle aboard huge barges towed behind seagoing tugboats. Tugs are a very efficient way to move a lot of cargo. With smaller crews and lower fuel costs, shippers can haul a lot of stuff for reasonable freight rates. These barges are massive, many over 300-feet long. They are basically just big sleds, loaded to the nuts with three or four levels of containers stacked on top of each other.

There's tons of fuel in tanks below deck. On top of the containers, huge beams are placed crosswise, and on top of those are motor homes, fishing boats, construction equipment, you name it. Everything is lashed down tight with heavy chains and binders.

An Alaskan freight company ran a route from Seattle up the Inside Passage, calling at Southeast Alaskan ports, as well as Cordova and Valdez, before crossing the Gulf of Alaska to Kodiak. It was a long, rugged supply line that was tough any time of the year, but just brutal in the winter.

The tug *Zephyr* had a crew of seven: a captain, two mates, one engineer, one cook and two deckhands. The *Zephyr* was an old Navy tug, 75-feet long with a single powerful engine. A huge tow winch filled the back deck with almost a quarter mile of two-inch steel tow cable wrapped on the drum. Top deck was the pilothouse forward, with a small connected stateroom for the captain. The lower deck had the galley forward, with a U-shaped settee surrounding a table that stretched the width of the room.

Immediately aft of the galley was a four-man bunk room, with two wooden bunks high—a set on each side—and lockers in the middle. Connecting with this compartment were two small rooms for a mate and the cook. Stepping out of the living quarters was open grating over the engine itself. (The tug is basically an engine with a few bunks attached.) The noise hit you like a fist the second the door was opened. That's where the toilet and shower were, a small room reached by walking on steel grating looking down on the engine.

Fueling the tug in Seattle, with Ricardo watching the gauge.

The tug was *loud*. We lived on top of the engine and when we were towing a barge at full speed, that engine was really cranking hard. There was kind of a deep throbbing scream that you felt in your bones. The quarters were relatively soundproofed but it was still hard to carry on conversations. On deck or in the engine room, even in the bathroom, it was necessary to wear foam earplugs with big "mickey mouse" ears, or heavy-duty ear protectors.

My first trip with this Alaskan tug and barge company was on the *Zephyr* on a cross-gulf trip in January, towing the freight barge *Mercury*. I thought I was fortunate to land the job. After it was too late, I discovered why the job was available.

The ride wasn't bad coming up the Inside Passage, as the route was protected from the open sea. After stops in Southeast Alaska, the route went west through Cross Sound out past Cape Spencer into the open waters of the gulf. In the winter our union required companies to pay a premium wage on any boat going west of Cape Spencer. Crew called it "blood money" for good reason.

As soon as we cleared Cape Spencer, the ass-kicking began. Man, it was one rough ride. Rolling violently from side to side and pitching up and down, it was all I could do to move around. The doors were all dogged down tight. There was no going outside as the boat was half underwater most of the time. Crew called it living in the belly of a whale. With the ribs of the ship showing on the interior, that was a pretty apt comparison. We had a unique appreciation for Jonah's ordeal.

Pounding along in some seriously large seas, the tug suddenly gave a big lurch forward. *Uh-oh.* Cap slowed down and we staggered to the back deck. We were shocked to see the winch drum empty of cable. The brake had failed and the lurch we felt was the end of the cable pulling out of the tow winch. The *Mercury*, now disconnected, was sailing away on her own.

That's not good. (This is a gross understatement.)

We can see the *Merc'*, loaded down heavy with cargo, bobbing like a cork and moving away as fast as the wind could blow her, heading for Japan. We gave chase and caught up with her, but now what?

Mercury "on the string" and busting waves.

Big freight barges have insanely heavy towing gear. On the bow is a heavy bridle made up of chain. Each link in the chain weighs 60 pounds. Where the ends of the bridle meet there is another 50 or 60 feet of that chain that connects to the tug's tow cable. This is called "surge gear" and the weight acts as a shock absorber as the towline rises and falls in heavy seas.

The tow cable is also extremely heavy and dips below the water on the way back to the barge. This is called the "catenary" and also acts as a shock absorber. Ocean tows are often strung out almost a quarter mile behind the tug, so the weight of the gear is considerable.

Barges have an emergency tow cable already rigged and tacked to the side with soft metal strips. At the stern of the barge, this emergency towline is connected to 100 feet of heavy-duty crab line and a large float called a "goofball." This trails the barge and allows a tug to come up behind with a grappling hook, catch the goofball, and hook up to the emergency towline. Then the tug veers off and as the soft metal strips tear off, the emergency towline peels off and the tow is retrieved.

That's the theory, anyway.

We got the goofball, which is easy to write about, but it took a couple hours of maneuvering while getting beat to paste and soaking wet. We got around to the front of the barge and took a strain, but with no heavy surge gear and a short towline with no catenary, the big seas caused the emergency line to snap like a kite string. And there goes the *Mercury* again, merrily sailing away. Meanwhile we're frantically pulling the busted cable in to keep it from fouling the prop. That would really put the cherry on the sundae.

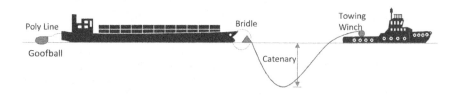

We didn't have any heavy line on the tug but there were coils of it on the barge. ON THE BARGE?? *But the barge is way over there!* Cap calls the crew together and says to me and Mark, the other deckhand, "I'm gonna try to nose up to the *Merc'* and you guys jump on and round up all the big hawser you can find." JUMP ON?? *Really?* Well, OK. When you put it like that it sounds easy...

Cap brings the tug around and approaches perpendicular to the barge. The barge is shooting up and down like a crazy elevator while we're moving up and down beside it, but out of sync, seconds later. Mark and I get up on the bow of the tug and when the barge comes swooping up, we just step off onto it as we go blasting skyward. *What a rush!* That was kind of exciting.

Now we're on this runaway barge in the middle of the Gulf of Alaska. Its rolling viciously, the cargo creaking and banging, and we see the tug pulling away. There's no time to worry how we're going to get back on the tug, although we're both thinking about that. Might as well get to work.

Mark and I start dragging big coils of polypropylene hawser—used for tie up—to the back of the barge. It's heavy and awkward and there is only an 18-inch wide walkway around the outside of the barge. Containers are stacked almost to the edge. The barge is rolling through a 60 or 70 degree arc so it's hard to stand. Going along the side, there are places where the safety rails have long since been torn off. There are also places where the cargo lashings don't line up with the vacant rails, so there's nothing to hang onto.

When the barge rolls down, we cling to the chains that are there. Then when the barge rolls the other way, we lay on the containers and shuffle across the bare spots before she rolls back. That was kind of exciting too.

Finally we had all the lines in one place and the tug creeps up to where we can take a heaving line and start feeding them over. We get the lines on the tug, and then here comes the big question: *How do we get back?* The bow of the tug comes to a point so it will be impossible to go back the same way we got on. It would be suicide to attempt it.

Mark and I are clinging to the chains, looking at each other and wondering if we are going to Japan with the *Mercury*.

The tug pulls up as close as they can get with all the thrashing and crashing going on, and they tell us we are going to have to jump. They piled a bunch of line in the bow for us to land on. *Wow*. This could get dicey. As the bow plunged up and down, we clung there trying to gauge the rolls and judge when we could go. Finally, I watch the bow climbing and just before it passes me, I jump. *Thank you, Jesus…I made it.*

Mark takes a while to get his nerve up, then he jumps, almost goes in the drink, but bounces off the rail and onto the pile of rope. *He makes it!* Whew, we're both safe, but jacked to the sky with adrenaline. So that was also kind of exciting.

We're still trailing the *Merc'* and Cap tells us the next plan: He's going to get as close as he can and one of us is going to put on a survival suit and swim around the barge's towline—which is hanging straight down, about a quarter mile of heavy cable—with a line, so we can pull the barge line close enough to hook up. REALLY?? I got hired in Sitka an hour before Mark so I have seniority. Mark's going.

Mark's in a survival suit with a line tied to his waist. Over the side he goes, swimming on his back toward the barge. But he's not making a whole lot of progress. Seas are still big so at times he's swimming uphill, and at other times we can't even see him. Every time the barge crashes down it pushes a big wave out in front of it, shooting Mark out and away like a ping pong ball. *There ain't no way Mark's gonna even get close.* I was worried he might get sucked under the barge. Turns out Mark was worried about that too.

"OK, guys, pull him back," Cap growls. He's mad at Mark for not trying harder. Guys start heaving, pulling Mark back to the tug. He's trying to yell at us and waving his arms wildly but we can't hear him. He's practically drowning by now anyway. Even though the tug's in neutral, the screw is still slowly turning and with every roll it comes clear of the water with a WHAP WHAP WHAP. Mark's afraid we're gonna pull him right into it. That's why he's freaking out.

We get Mark on board and he is terrified and *pissed off!* He starts screaming at Earl, the captain. There's lots of profanity. He's telling Earl what an idiot he is, and that as soon as we hit Kodiak he's quitting. I don't blame him. Mark was pretty excited.

Earl says, "OK, let's take a break. And then Lonnie, you can give it a try." I give him an amazed stare. I say, "Earl, you can fire me right now. I'll even work the rest of the trip knowing I'm fired. But I'm not going over the side in a survival suit." Earl grumbles and fumes, mumbling something about following orders. But there is not a chance in hell of me changing my mind and he knows it.

All we can do is follow the *Mercury* and hope the weather calms down. We follow her for five days until the wind sends her close enough to shore for the dragging cable to slow her down. Once that happened and the weather dropped, we were able to get close enough to retrieve the towline and reattach it to the tug. Again, easy to write about, but it took about 48 straight hours of wrenching on huge cable clamps, trying to make an eye in two-inch cable that would hold up when towing a barge.

We would wrench one as tight as we could get it using cheater bars. Then as soon as we tightened up the next one, the first one would now be loose. And so on and so forth for hours and hours. At one point I noticed Earl, who had a history of heart issues, putting a nitro pill under his tongue. I thought, *Oh, hell yeah. Let's throw a medevac into this floating circus.*

We finally made Kodiak, a week late but with all our cargo intact, and then sat around for a couple days while the winch got fixed. After the last week we had, that was kind of anticlimactic. Almost boring.

Mark quit.

I signed on for another trip. I thought this offshore towing stuff was pretty exciting!

15

Knock Me Over with a Feather

Winter comes early on the Gulf of Alaska. By October gales are blowing steadily down out of the Bering Sea. On the ocean, off Baranof Island, the seas grow to black mountains. The wind never stops. Neither do the commercial fishermen. No fish means no money, so they go out, fair weather or foul. They have to, it's how they support their families. Some never return.

It was a typical in-port evening. The 56-man crew of the U.S. Coast Guard cutter *Clover* (WLB-292), a 1940s-vintage buoy tender, were scattered around the sleepy fishing village of Sitka. Some were at home with their families, but most of the young guys were hanging out at the Pioneer Bar. It was a nasty night outside and we were warm and happy where we were.

Our mellow mood was rudely interrupted when the *Clover's* whistle began to echo across the harbor: Morse code letter "P" (phonetic alphabet Papa). Dot-dash-dash-dot. Short long long short. That's the signal for emergency recall. *Crew to the boat immediately!* We knew the ship's van was on the way to collect us, so we chugged our beers, threw on our parkas, and headed out the door.

The *Alaskan Star*, a local fishing boat with four men aboard, was in trouble 15 miles out at sea. A line was tangled in their prop, jamming the rudder as well. She had no way to steer. The fear was she would get broadside to the huge waves and capsize, which was a very real possibility. Their crew was panicked, you could hear it in their voices over the radio. They were begging for help and giving us messages for their families in case they didn't make it. There was no time to lose.

The saying in the Coast Guard was "you have to go out, but nobody says you have to come back." Funny, the recruiter never mentioned that. But it's our job, so out we go, "All Ahead Full" (speed). Or as the chief called it, "All Ahead Frantic."

It was just a brutal night on the ocean. Huge seas were breaking with white teeth that the wind sent stinging into our faces. The lights of town disappeared immediately and in the pilothouse (the bridge) it was inky black, except for the dim red lights on the radar equipment. The only sounds were murmured commands, the crackle and hiss of the radios, and the stomach-turning retching of the helmsman, "Spanky" LeCroix, puking up the two Pioneer Bar hotdogs he had inhaled on his way out the door. Over all that was the incredible din of a large ship being beaten like a drum. Shadowy figures staggered from radar to chart table while the silhouette of the captain was unmoving, staring out the front window.

The ship was airborne half the time and underwater the rest. The noise was unbelievable and when it smashed down into the trough of the waves it hit so hard it rattled our bones. We were all thinking about the guys on the *Alaskan Star* and praying we would find them still afloat.

We arrived on scene and it was wild. The *Alaskan Star* was lit up with every light they had and it was just being hammered. We could see damage, but she was still upright. As she flew up the side of a huge wave we could see a bundle of rope dangling from her screw (prop). She was at the mercy of the sea and was getting the worst of it. We weren't doing much better but at least we could steer. Sort of.

Captain maneuvered us upwind of the *Star* so we could try to get a line down to her. But one minute we could see her and the next she would be gone, up and over the next sea. She was up, we were down, we were on top of a giant wave, and she went careening down the backside. There was terrible visibility, unbelievable seas, and a vicious wind.

Our gunner's mate, Craig, had a line-throwing gun up on the bow. He had two guys clinging to his legs so he could stand, but they were being tossed around like rag dolls. BANG. Craig let a shot go. A weight flew out of the gun trailed by 800 feet of light line, trying to get it into the *Alaskan Star's* rigging so her crew could haul over our towline. But the wind grabbed Craig's line and blew it right back over the *Clover*. Cap maneuvered the ship around a bit and BANG...Craig tries again. Same result. No joy.

We are trying to keep our searchlights on the *Star*, but as we were snap-rolling through a 90-degree arc, the light beams could only catch her briefly. The captain yelled to me, "Calloway, get up on the roof and fire up the clacker." The clacker was a bright spotlight with shutters on the front that was used to send Morse code by "clacking" a lever on the side. By holding the lever down, the shutters would stay open and in a pinch it could be used as another searchlight. But fuck me runnin'...THE ROOF?? *I don't wanna go up on the roof!*

It was not my option though, so up I go. I could hardly stand up and was soaking wet almost immediately. We were going up and down the steep waves so fast my stomach was constantly in my throat. I needed to hold on to the clacker lever just to stay on the ship.

I got the light on and it shot out a thick beam of illumination. I could get brief glimpses of the *Star* but holding the light on her was impossible. My beam would hit her as we blew past, up and over a huge sea, down and under the next. It was a lot of work trying to keep swinging the light to try to stay with her. My beam was all over the sky.

Suddenly out of the blackness a shadow appeared in front of my light. An instant later, before I could register what was happening, the shadow smashed into my light, putting it out in a loud POP and a shower of broken glass. At the same time, something large came flopping over the top of the busted light, hitting me full in the face and knocking me backwards off my feet. Flat on my back and a bit dazed, I was aware of something thrashing around near me. It was a pelagic albatross with at least a seven-foot wing span. It must have been disoriented by the lights slicing through the dark sky and smashed full speed into me and my light.

There was so much noise that me hitting the deck didn't even register down in the pilothouse. I was more than a little freaked out and the captain was hollering to get the light back on, RIGHT NOW! Well, that wasn't gonna happen anytime soon, so I jumped down to the bridge to explain. When I went in the door, everybody looked at me in shock. I didn't realize it but I was a fearsome sight, coming out of the night covered in bird blood and with feathers stuck to my beard. Guys told me later that I scared the crap out of them. I was jabbering about a bird and pointing up at the busted light. They thought I had lost my mind.

About that time, BANG…*success!* Craig managed to get a line on the *Star* and her crew started hauling over the towline. That wasn't an easy evolution either and things got real busy on the bridge. My destroyed light and I were immediately forgotten, so I just got cleaned up and went back to work.

The hook-up was quite a feat in itself, but after another hour of rigorous deck work and impressive seamanship, we got the *Alaskan Star* in tow. We could all breathe again. Guys on the *Star* were so relieved. They kept thanking us. We didn't need thanks but were certainly glad they were safe. We knew it didn't always end this well.

Heading back to town towing the *Star* was a long slow trip, still getting continuously slammed. Around daybreak things were as under control as they could be, and the captain finally asked me what the hell happened last night. I told him to come with me and see. We went up the ladder to the bridge roof and there was a huge dead bird. There were feathers, blood and broken glass all over, frozen to the deck. He was speechless for a minute, then with a low whistle laughed, "Daaamnnn. Ya don't see that every day."

I sure hope I never do again.

16

Zing!

Southeast Alaska is the home of the Tongass National Forest. For 50 years the National Forest Service sold logs from the Tongass to the Japanese owners of the pulp mills in Sitka and Ketchikan. Alaska Lumber and Pulp bought vast quantities of Sitka spruce and other timber for processing and shipment to Japan.

This industry created many jobs and was an economic force in the area. Logging companies, fuel companies, equipment suppliers, mechanics, and tugboat outfits hired to tow rafts of cut logs to the mills, all benefited.

Logs were cut to a uniform length, banded into bundles with steel straps, and slid into the ocean to holding pens. There, small one-man tugs called "boom tugs" or "log broncs" would push the bundles into "booms." These logs were huge and a bundle would easily be 10 feet or more in diameter, made up of several logs.

Towing the log raft through town, praying
we don't hit anything expensive.

A "boom" was formed by a series of large logs called "boom sticks" chained together, end to end, into a large rectangle. One end was opened and the bundles were pushed in, floating free but constrained by the boom sticks. When the boom was full of bundles, the end was closed off with another boom stick. When several booms were fastened together with "boom chains," it formed a "raft" and could stretch for a quarter mile.

When a raft was ready, a tugboat would be dispatched to hook on and tow it to the mill. Usually there would be two tugs involved, with the bigger one in front doing the actual towing and the other tug tied off to the stern of the raft, called a "tail-boat." The tail-boat's job was to help guide the long tow around the bends and twists in the waterways leading to the mill. If any parts or supplies were needed—maybe groceries or a change of crew—the tail-boat could untie, run into town and be back, while the lead tug thrashed slowly along.

By the 1980s, logging was slowing down and there wasn't steady log-towing work for the big companies, so tug owners would get a one-time contract for a tow. They recruited whatever crew were in town at the time to go grab the raft and bring it in. With my week-on/week-off schedule on the Alaska ferries, I was often able to jump on a log tow for a few days and make some extra cash.

It was a lot of fun and usually pretty laid back. When tail-boating, since we were tied up to the raft itself, it was possible to put a pair of spiked sandals on your feet and go for a walk on the raft as it churned along. The raft wasn't solid, just a mass of floating bundles, so a walk meant jumping from bundle to bundle while the bundles bobbed and bounced along.

It could get a little exciting because of how the bundles moved. The way back to the boat was never the same. Sometimes there would be open water as the bundles floated around. You had to either go another way or vault over the opening using a pike pole. Miss and you would be in the water between the bundles, being ground to hamburger.

Danny, on the raft.

At times there might be more than one raft ready, or the weather would get too rough to tow. There were a few protected bays used to stash a raft until a tug could retrieve it. The raft would be shackled off to a permanent mooring buoy or even tied off to trees on the beach.

My buddy, Rick, ran a small business, Kruzof Towing, with a tug named *Rocket*. His father-in-law, whom we called "Grampa," ran Chatham Straits Towing with his tug *Misty Dawn*. These guys were small operators but kept busy with the jobs the big outfits didn't want to mess with. Even though they were separate companies they often towed rafts together, the *Misty Dawn* towing in front and *Rocket* tail-boating.

Rocket tied off in the tail-boat position.

One time Rick called me to go out with him and Grampa to retrieve a raft that was stored in a distant bay. Cool by me. Weather was good and it sounded like a fun trip. Off we went.

We got to the bay and discovered a big problem. Southeast Alaska had good size tides twice a day, often raising and lowering the water level 12 feet or more. Twice a month there would be a tide called a "spring" tide that was higher than normal. There had recently been a spring tide and the higher water had put one end of the log raft high and dry on the beach. Since the following tides were smaller they didn't refloat the whole raft.

We could wait a couple weeks and see if the next spring tide would get it back in the water, but Rick and Grampa had already burned the fuel and paid the crews to come all this way. Grampa figured he could pull the raft off the beach with the *Misty Dawn*.

He brought 600 feet of yellow polypropylene hawser, or "poly," which was big stuff, four inches in diameter. I didn't even know they made poly that large. Thank God it already had an eye in one end, because I sure didn't relish having to splice this stuff. Attached to the eye was a shackle that must have weighed 35 pounds, with a pin the size of a baby's arm. This was some serious gear.

We tied the *Rocket* off to the wet end of the raft and took the skiff out to *Misty Dawn*. Then we picked up the shackle and the end of the line. Poly line floats so we just towed it in while Grampa's deckhands, Butch and Danny, paid out slack.

To keep log rafts in some kind of rectangular shape while being towed, there are heavy-duty cables, called "swifters," that are run across a raft from side to side over the booms. Spaced out over the length of the raft, these are what really hold the raft together.

Misty Dawn pulling hard around a bend.

We dragged the line over the beached section of the raft and shackled it to a swifter. Grampa throttled up the *Misty Dawn* and took a strain. There were lots of loud snaps and pops as the logs started to shift. Rick and I are standing on the raft as there was nowhere else to go. There was absolutely nowhere to run if things went south, so why worry? What could go wrong?

Grampa was really putting the hammer down. Black smoke's belching out of the tug's stack and the whole boat is heeling over as the screw took a big bite.

Poly line will stretch a lot under load, and this stuff was starting to look like kite string. Grampa let off the gas and the line started pulling the boat backwards. He let it slack down a bit then powered up again. Things were starting to move under us and Rick and I were getting a little nervous.

A couple more back and forth jerks and Grampa lets the line sag way back. He took a flying run again, really blasting along, and comes up on the end of the line. The whole raft starts groaning. There's nothing but white foam behind the boat as he slams the throttle to the stops.

Rick and I are on either side of the swifter. We're watching the tension, feeling the raft cracking, and just generally having a good time, yucking it up. The hawser is stretching way out again, even more than before if that's possible, and it looks like it's beginning to smoke.

Suddenly with a loud BANG, the swifter snaps. Basically a big rubber band, the poly line retracts instantly, shooting that 35-pound shackle between Rick and me like a cannonball. We felt the air move as it blew by our heads. The raft crashes back down and we both end up on our asses.

Jumping back up, we watch the shackle sailing through the air back toward the *Misty Dawn*, and it's still climbing. The yellow poly line is curling after it, and the shackle's really moving...directly toward its other end, which was firmly tied to the tug. Remember high school science? *For every action there is an equal and opposite reaction.* Well, there was one hell of a lot of energy suddenly released and it was definitely reacting in an opposite direction!

Grampa on the *Misty Dawn*.

We could see Butch and Danny on the stern shading their eyes and watching the projectile heading right for them. They suddenly realized what was coming and almost smashed into each other trying to get off the back deck. It was comical to watch.

The shackle sailed over the tug's stern, trailing the poly line. As it crossed the stern, some of the slack line snagged on the upper deck rail. This immediately changed the direction the shackle was flying and multiplied its kinetic power.

Pivoting down with savage force, it splintered through the top of the tug like it was butter.

Grampa about had the big one. Turning shakily from his position behind the wheel, he found himself face to face and bare inches away from the shackle, now swinging gently back and forth in the wreckage of the pilothouse roof. Yards of yellow poly hawser draped over the tug like a Christmas decoration.

It seemed to take forever, but it actually happened in the blink of an eye. Rick and I stood there, bug-eyed and open-mouthed, still in shock over our close call. But it was kind of cool to see.

We got a call on the radio from Grampa. In a quivering voice, he said, "Shut 'er down boys, we're headin' for town. I need a drink."

Damn straight, Grampa. Ditto on the drink.

We went back out on the next spring tide and the beached raft floated off the beach as pretty as you please. This time, a big piece of steel plate covered the roof of the *Misty Dawn*.

Grampa wasn't taking any more chances.

Speaking of blowing my mind, there was another logging technique that I thought was mega-cool. As I mentioned, the mill in Sitka made pulp to send to Japan to make fiberboard, and we towed many rafts of logs to the mill. The Canadians, however, were a bit more clever.

They would show up with a huge ship, the deck loaded crossways with logs.

Canadian log ship preparing to unload at the pulp mill.

We would take two tugs out and tie off to each end of the ship. The ship would shut off her engines and start pumping water into the ballast tank on the downhill side to heel her over.

The ship heeling over.

When she tipped far enough, the logs would slide off with a ROAR, and the ship would shoot sideways across the bay.

There they all go, even snapping the tug's line holding the ship. Never a dull moment!

The logs would almost disappear underwater, then pop back up in the air and float. Our tugs were there to keep the dead ship under control.

Love that Canadian efficiency: three days to load,
10 seconds to dump.

I always loved going on these tug jobs and would almost have worked them for free. As one old shipmate used to say, "Sometimes this job is more fun than God should allow!" *Amen, brother.*

17

The Circus Comes to Kodiak

"The Gulf of Alaska is the cradle of storms that blow across North America. It has no mercy on you when it really gets going."
—An Oil Tanker Captain

The Alaska Marine Highway system is a nautical transportation system operated by the state to provide public transportation between the many island towns, villages and cities in the watery archipelagos of Southeast and Southwest Alaska. The mainliners, M/V *Columbia*, M/V *Matanuska*, M/V *Malaspina* and M/V *Taku* run weekly routes from Seattle/Bellingham, Washington to Skagway, Alaska, hitting all the ports up and back on a seven-day turnaround. The M/V *Aurora* and the M/V *LeConte* service the far flung native villages of Hoonah, Angoon, Kake and Metlakatla.

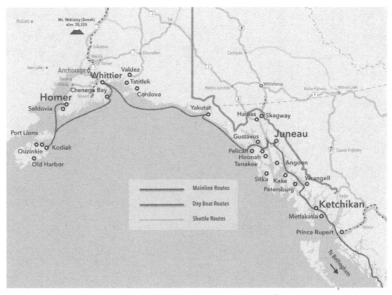

Map courtesy of Alaska Marine Highway System

These "feeder ferries" pick up passengers and take them to the nearest town, sit dockside all day while people do their shopping, doctor appointments, etc., and then take them back home. They keep moving down the line to the next village and do the same thing. All these vessels operate in the relatively protected waters of the Inside Passage.

The M/V *Tustumena*, also known as the "Trusty Tusty" or the "Blue Canoe"—or more accurately, the "Dramamine Express"—ran the Big Boy route. This went straight across the Gulf of Alaska from Seward to Kodiak, a 20-hour run in good weather, a never-ending nightmare in bad. In reality, it was almost always bad. It's just a matter of degree.

Twice a month in the summer, she ran a seven-day round trip out the Aleutian Chain of Islands to Dutch Harbor. Called by the crew "going out the chain" (and referring to themselves as the "chain gang"), the *Tustumena* stopped at the villages of Chignik, Sand Point, King Cove, Cold Bay, False Pass and Akutan, before arriving in Dutch Harbor, or "Dutch," a lonely outpost of crab boats and WW2 ruins on the Bering Sea.

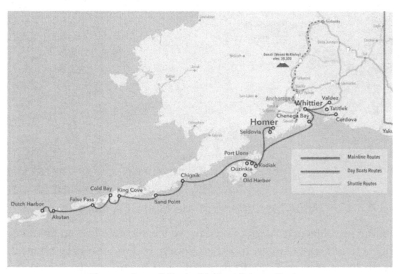

Map courtesy of Alaska Marine Highway System

In the winter, weather-wise, there would be no mercy. Often, outward bound from Homer, Alaska on the weekly run to Kodiak, the *Tustumena* would be feeling the gulf's wrath. Climbing nearly vertically up a huge sea only to plunge straight down into the dark trough between the oncoming monsters, she would only make four or five miles an hour and get her ass kicked in the bargain. Just business as usual for the only ocean-rated ship in the Alaska ferry fleet.

She ran on a schedule, so waiting out weather was never an option. Coming into Kodiak, the captain would slow outside of town so the deck gang could hose the coating of vomit off the shipside facing the dock. Didn't want to scare the waiting return passengers. There was always vomit, confirming the *Tustumena's* other nickname: the "Vomit Comet."

Many passengers, accustomed to the sedate crossings on the Washington State ferries or a sun-splashed voyage to Mackinac Island, would be bug-eyed and praying, puking their guts out before she was halfway across the gulf. Whether you called it "chirping" or "feeding the fish," as the crew did, it was a hell of a ride.

M/V *Tustumena* in the Gulf of Alaska

Pulling into Homer, Alaska one day, we were greeted by an amazing sight. Waiting to board was a circus. It was an honest-to-God traveling carnival, complete with lions and tigers and bears. *Oh my!* Colorful vans, semi-trailers and vehicles of every description were lined up on the dock. There were trucks with cages containing monkeys and who knew what else. And in one large truck, an elephant's trunk could be seen testing the harbor air.

The *Tustumena* carried everything and anything that could roll or be dragged onto the elevator and lowered below to the car deck. Army tanks for the Alaska National Guard, a float plane minus the wings, and once, a trailer full of llamas on their way to an outfitter on Unalaska Island. But until that day, never a circus.

Right away we knew there was going to be a problem. The vehicle elevator was 40-feet long. It dropped to the lower deck where it could swivel, like a turntable, to put cars on either side of the ship for proper balance. If a vehicle pulling a trailer or a commercial semi-trailer longer than 40 feet wanted to board, the crew had to do a "double shuffle."

**The elevator for loading the car deck,
with First Mate Ole on the dock.**

First you had to back the trailer onto the elevator and disconnect it. Then the tow vehicle moves off. The elevator goes down and another rig hooks on down in the hold and backs the trailer into position. Getting off, the process was reversed. It was time-consuming on a good day, but there were usually only a few double shuffles and the commercial semi-drivers were expert at this.

Here's where the problem lay with our circus. Before the tow vehicle disconnects on the elevator, either a tongue jack or, in the case of semi-trailers, the supporting "landing gear" has to be cranked down to support the tongue and enable the next tow vehicle to hook up quickly.

This circus was kind of a rag-tag gypsy outfit and their trucks had seen better days. Many had not been disconnected from their trailers for years, if ever. There was typically no need, as they always traveled by highway. But this highway had length restrictions. On more than a few vehicles the landing gear was either completely frozen or missing entirely.

The crew started down the line of trucks soaking the rusty metal in Break-Free cleaner/lubricant and WD-40, hoping to free up some of the gear. In some cases it worked. In too many it did not.

The only thing to do was get cracking. The ship had heavy rolling jacks that were used to shore up semi-trailers, in addition to the landing gear, for the often violent crossing. These were brought to the elevator and one by one the ancient rigs were broken apart, jacked up and stowed in the hold. It took seemingly forever, with all hands called out to assist.

The bummer we all knew was coming was that the exact same thing would have to be done when disembarking the circus in Kodiak. And then twice more for their return trip. We were definitely earning our pay with this bunch. It was gonna be a long trip.

Finally we got everything stowed and lashed down tight. As usual, the weather report called for high winds and big seas. The *Tustumena* was equipped with hydraulic wing stabilizers in the hull that could be activated to help slow the roll. Unfortunately these didn't help when the ship was airborne!

The car deck looked like Noah's Ark and it sounded like the ark must have, too. All manner of squeaks, roars, chatter and trumpeting could be heard throughout the ship. As we left the protection of the bay and hit the open ocean, the ship really started to move around. And the animals didn't like that one bit. The din from the car deck increased in volume.

The ship was doing what it was designed to do: travel while staying afloat. But it was really covering some ground to do that, including in the vertical plane, as we soared and slammed over and under huge seas. Lying in my bunk, one minute I would be weightless and lifted off the mattress, and the next I'd be pushed down hard on the springs. This went on hour after hour. With that and the circus animals screaming in fear right outside the door to crew quarters, nobody was sleeping. The animals sure weren't.

It was 3:00 a.m. and I was on watch in the wheelhouse. Steve was on the wheel and fighting to stay somewhat on course. Steering a specific compass course was impossible. The mate Phil's instructions were, "Keep heading as much southwest as you can hold her." I had just finished my shift on the wheel and I was whipped, slumped in the lookout chair.

We had the stereo cranked up listening to Pink Floyd "Dark Side of the Moon." This was partly to drown out the noise from the car deck but mainly because that was our go-to tunes for bad weather. The worse it got, the louder the volume. D.S.O.T.M. was awesome music for zooming up the face of big waves and then going weightless as the ship blew over the top and dropped like a rock down into the trough.

There was not much conversation, just an exclamation now and then when a particularly big one hit. "Jesus, did you see that?" or the old standby, "Holy shit!" was uttered in a reverent tone as green water broke over the wheelhouse, covering the windows.

Ned, the night watchman, burst through the door in a panic. "Mate Mate Mate, there's trouble on the car deck! The elephant's hurt. They need help!"

I jumped out of my chair and told Phil, "I got it!" as I followed Ned off the bridge. We were both bouncing off the walls as we staggered down the passageway.

Driving the Dramamine Express.

The car deck was bedlam. All the animals were in full cry, but above it all could be heard the shrill trumpeting of an elephant in distress. It stopped me in my tracks for a second, but I kept following Ned. We went weaving through the chained-down trucks and slipping on the huge puddles of assorted animal feces and urine now covering the deck.

The elephant was in a large truck with slat sides and a big door in the middle. In his frenzy and fear he had managed to kick the door so hard that it bent out at the bottom and his foot had become wedged. The more he struggled the louder he screamed. The whole ship was awake—not that they weren't already—hearing a sound none of us had ever heard outside a Tarzan movie.

The trainer was there trying to calm him, with little success. He told me the

111

elephant's name was Mickey. I thought, *Hey Mickey, you're a long way from the jungle.*

Ned was a retired logger and was an expert about rigging and tackle. He looked the truck over and started shouting instructions. We got a cable and come-along rigged to the bottom of the door and Billy, the oiler, started cranking on it, bending the bottom of the door out even more. "Red" and "Chainsaw," the other deckhands, started jacking the floor under the door for stability.

The pressure was lessening but Mickey's foot was too far out the door to get traction. Grabbing a long iron bar, the trainer and I put it under his foot and heaved to give him just a tiny bit of leverage. This all would have been tough enough under normal circumstances, but we were still just hammering through the ocean and could hardly stand up. And as I mentioned, the deck was slippery with exotic animal effluvia. Tiger piss is nasty stuff.

As we worked to free him, Mickey's trunk was out between the slats and whipping back and forth frantically over our heads. The trainer was wild-eyed. He yelled, "Keep your head down and watch out for his trunk. He killed a pony once."

I had long since accepted that I might someday lose my life in a shipwreck, and never worried about that. But to get decapitated by a crazed elephant in the middle of the Gulf of Alaska was just too bizarre to consider. Besides, the pony was probably an asshole and had it coming.

We finally got Mickey freed without any mayhem to the crew and, although still agitated, he seemed to settle down a bit. We were a mess, all covered in elephant shit from sliding around under Mickey's truck, and pumped full of adrenaline. Red's eyes were rolling around like marbles. I'm pretty sure mine were too.

Things calmed down a bit by morning and the animals quieted down, either getting used to the motion or so damn exhausted they all passed out. It was the same with the passengers.

Limping into Kodiak we were greeted by a crowd on the dock. They were expecting a triumphant circus parade disembarking the ship. Schools had been let out to see the spectacle. What they got was a line of bedraggled and vomit-stained performers stumbling down the gangway, some actually kissing the pavement.

One truck at a time, they painfully pulled out of the hold, each taking at least a half hour or more to haul out. The animals were listless and in some cases still passed out. The crew, dead on our feet, were moving like zombies.

The only happy one was Mickey. His truck came off with him cheerfully munching on peanuts. I think he winked at me.

18

Burn, Baby, Burn

Admit it, we've all screwed up. I certainly have, and when I do I make sure it's a doozy. But I gotta own it. No apologies or excuses. As much as I'd often like to, I can't rewrite history.

So it's November 1984, and I'm heading back to Michigan after a three month stretch on the Alaska State Ferry, *Tustumena*. I had a pocketful of cash and a desire to sleep in a bed that wasn't moving. The main reason for my trip was to see my family and pick up a 1978 Jeep CJ7 I had stashed in a friend's garage. I planned to take it back to my home in Sitka, Alaska. Even though there were only seven miles of road out each end of town on Baranof Island, having wheels would make a huge improvement in my lifestyle.

After a fun visit in Michigan, I headed west. I really enjoyed the trip, travelling all by myself. After months on a ship with people in my face morning, noon and night the solitude was intoxicating. I had some brake problems in Idaho, but I was only one state away from Seattle so just planned to drag my feet, Fred Flintstone-style, until I could make the coast and get them fixed. There were a few dicey moments near Spokane, but finally, into the Emerald City I rolled— no soles on my shoes, but still intact.

Since I was an employee of the State of Alaska, I could get my vehicle on the ferry for free. Unfortunately, the next boat was four days out. I got my brakes fixed day one, then had three more days to kill. I got a room at second-rate hotel on the edge of downtown Seattle and settled in to wait for the boat.

It was November, so nothing much was going on and the weather sucked. I was on the third floor at the hotel and I was one of the very few guests. The only people I saw were the desk clerk—who was kind of a dickhead—and a Vietnamese gardener/janitor named Tuan. He was alright. I got the impression Tuan hated the desk clerk too, so we had a bond right away. He helped me move my gear.

Man, I was bored. I cruised around town a bit but nothing really grabbed me and it wouldn't stop raining. So I spent a lot of time in my room, just watching the tube and taking naps. I thought the boat would never get there.

At one point, I stopped in at a marine supply store just to look around. I owned a sweet Boston Whaler in Sitka and was always on the lookout for new boat stuff. They were having a sale on flare guns, a necessary part of every Alaskan gear box, so I bought one. It was a nice one, too, this little twelve-gauge flare pistol: blaze orange, red magnesium flares, 30-second burn time, shells as big as my thumb. Oh yeah, pretty manly stuff!

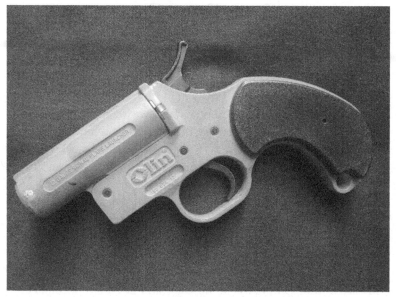

The culprit.

Then I'm back at the hotel, still waiting for the boat, still bored out of my skull. I may have had a few beers. Well, no *maybe* about it. It was "Vitamin R" (Ranier) and "It's Oly Time" (Olympia). I love the Pacific Northwest!

Idly watching TV, I thought I should check out the flare gun. *What a great idea!* I pulled it out and started fiddling with it. Click, click, click…I pointed it all over the room and popped off imaginary rounds. I even took out a shell and tried it for fit. Yup, it fits. I took the shell out and set it aside. I *thought* I took it out, that is. You can see where this is going.

Awhile later, and definitely a few beers later, I picked the flare gun up again. I pointed it at the TV, pointed it at the door, then pointed it up into the corner of the room and squeezed the trigger. BOOM!! *There's a surprise!* The shell was still in it.

A big ball of fire blasts out of the gun, hits the ceiling and bounces into the corner of the room. Man, it's bright—a blazing red ball—putting out clouds of thick red smoke. (You want the Coast Guard to see you 50 miles away, after all.)

I am frozen in shock for about two seconds. Then either my shipboard training or my sense of self-preservation kicks in. I vote for the latter.

The smoke alarm is wailing and I can't see. The first thing I do is tear that damn smoke alarm right off the wall to shut it the hell up. Then I jam a towel under the door to stop the smoke from going out in the hall.

I go stumbling toward the window in the blind. Meanwhile, the flare is still burning merrily in the corner. On the way by, thinking fast—or hardly thinking—I threw my goose down vest in the corner to try to smother the flare. That was a great move, as it immediately bursts into flames and melts, adding the smell of burning feathers to the already toxic brew I'm trying not to breathe.

I throw open the window and the draft immediately sucks a thick column of dark red smoke out the window. I see Tuan down in the parking lot. He waves and continues raking. I guess in Vietnam burning hotels are a common sight.

With a last hiss, the flare burns out. Thirty seconds seemed like an hour. I'm hyperventilating like a winded rabbit, my heart beating out of my chest.

Now the smoke's gone, Tuan's still raking, and I survey the damage. There's a big dent in the popcorn ceiling where the flare hit before bouncing into the corner. Thank God it didn't go all the way through or there would have been no more hotel.

The wall was covered in soot and looked like I had sacrificed a virgin. But I was in Seattle by the docks, so there weren't any of those to be found. There was also a big melted spot on the carpet, plus the wispy remains of burning goose down floating in the air.

Aw, crap. They have my credit card. Guess I'll have to own up. I call the desk and the dickhead answers. I tell him I've had a little problem in room 332 and he may want to drop by. He shows up and about has a stroke. He starts stammering and moaning that the boss will be mad, and that he will need at least three contractors to fix all the damage. He says I'm probably going to jail. He bolts out of the room to call his boss.

Now, my brother, Tim, is a world class MacGyver. When I get in a jam, the first thing I think of is: WWTD, or What Would Tim Do? I most definitely didn't want to go to the King County jail, so I got to work.

The dent in the popcorn ceiling was easy. I mixed Ultrabright toothpaste with the ends of a couple cotton swabs and made a spackle. After I filled the hole, you couldn't even see it. I put some shampoo in the ice bucket and scrubbed the soot down off the wall using a wool sock. After all my deckie time, I can "soogee" like a pro. By the time I got done, you couldn't even tell there had been a fire.

Then I went next door to the maid's locker and got a vacuum cleaner and some air freshener. I sucked up all the remaining charred feathers and made the air smell like a pine forest after a spring rain. The main remaining problems were: 1) the destroyed smoke alarm, and 2) the melted spot on the carpet. I took the whole smoke alarm assembly off and hid it in my bag. Then I moved furniture around slightly to cover the worst of the carpet and a dark spot on the wall. It really didn't look too bad.

About a half hour later, there was a knock on the door. It's the manager with the dickhead in tow. He comes in and looks around suspiciously. "Hey, buddy," I greet him. "Glad you're here. I had a large candle burning and it fell on the floor. Before I could get to it some carpet got melted. I'd be happy to pay for the damage."

The room does look pretty good. He turns to the dickhead and starts reaming him a new one, telling him he was at a family dinner and had to leave because the dork told him the motel was burning down. *Dammit, my cheap-ass son-in-law was springing for crab!* The dickhead's stammering, "But but but," and backing out into the hall.

I tell the boss, "I don't know what that guy's problem is. But he was treating Tuan like crap too. How about I give you 50 bucks to fix the carpet?"

"That's cool," he says. "Sorry for the misunderstanding."

"No problem," I say. "Oh, by the way, this room didn't even have a smoke alarm."

I move to another second-rate hotel and spend the next two days waiting for the boat, bored again.

19

Beef Jerky and Bridge Diving

For the crew, living conditions on the U.S. Coast Guard cutter *Clover* were worse than in a divey motel. Far worse. At least in a "no-tell-motel," one could be reasonably certain of a single room and some privacy. Not so on the *Clover*.

***Clover* with Mount Edgecumbe in the background.**

The *Clover* (WLB-292) was a 180-foot buoy tender, called a "Buck-80." Also used as a Search and Rescue (SAR) platform, she was designed for ATON (Aids TO Navigation) work. With her hull painted black except for the Coast Guard "racing stripe" on the bow, the *Clover*, or "Sea (C)-Lover" to her crew, was a workhorse. She performed her missions well, but to say she was short on amenities would be a wild understatement.

With a crew of 56, living space was limited. The five officers had single rooms aft. There were separate berthing areas for the five or six chief petty officers (E-7s), and the five or six first class petty officers (E-6s). The remaining

40 or so crew, seamen apprentices (E-2s) up to second class petty officers (E-5s), all bunked in "crew berthing," more commonly referred to as "the tank."

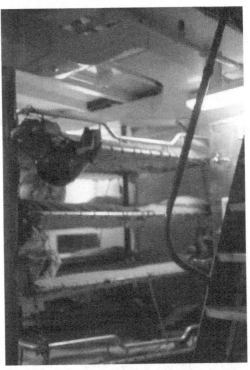

A stack in the tank.

The tank was in the very belly of the ship. Accessed by stairs (ladders) at each end, to enter it you "laid below." There were no toilet facilities so the crew had to go up (above) to find the bathrooms (heads). Bunks (racks) were arranged in eight pods, four-high (a stack) and two stacks adjoining. A rack was canvas lashed to a metal frame with a thin mattress laid on, and with barely two and a half feet of vertical clearance between the shelves. Some tattered material called "privacy drapes"(or "jerk curtains," by the crew) hung from some of the frames.

The only thing that separated you from the guy in the opposite "shelf" on your level was a steel bar. If you wanted to read a book it was by flashlight laying on your side. All the racks were hinged to the center posts so they could be raised flat or "triced up." Generally, only the bottom rack in the stack was required to be triced each morning so the compartment cleaner could sweep the deck.

With little or no working ventilation and absolutely no A/C, the air in the tank could be cut with a knife. With the combined smells of body odor, bad breath, farts and vomit hanging in the air, at times it was possible to actually see the atmosphere. That was *in port*. When we were underway and the doors (hatches) were closed, the vomit level arose from seasickness instead of drunkenness and it was a whole other thing. It was like a bad never-ending camping trip, in a tent with 40 of your homeless friends.

My first night on the *Clover*, being the new guy, the only vacant rack was the top one on an eight-pod. Climbing a ladder to get in, I found myself laying with my head inches from several of the ship's service pipes. I couldn't help but compare it with the spacious two-man room with bath and *two* portholes I had just left on my last Great Lakes iron ore boat.

I quickly learned that good racks were gold. If a guy had a premium rack, mainly meaning one on the bottom of a stack and close to the ladder—both for a bit more fresh air and ease of escape in a disaster—he would sell it to the highest bidder before he left. Kind of like in prison.

After two nights sleeping amongst the plumbing, with water (?) gurgling through the pipe inches from my face every time someone flushed a toilet, and with the bad air rising and enveloping me like a cloud, I was ready to desert. Luckily, one of the guys was leaving and I bought his rack for $75. It was the best rack in the tank and the best money I ever spent. I would have gone higher. Much higher.

My $75 rack on the bottom.

Not more than half a mile away was the sparkling new Coast Guard Air Station Sitka, featuring beautiful dormitories built for the helicopter crews (called "rotor-heads" or "Airedales"). Of course officers had off-base housing, but their crew—from the newest "boot recruit" to the senior petty officers—lived in kingly splendor. They had two-man rooms rivaling upscale college dorms, complete with a private bath and shower. Plus a huge rec room with a big screen TV and even their own bar. It was impossible not to compare this with the tank.

Generally, the rotor-heads worked a 40-hour week and, except for duty days, were off and home each evening. The boys on the *Clover* were underway and gone from home an average of 270 days a year, and even when we were in port the rule was "on board, on duty." This meant that whenever we were off work and on the boat (where we lived), we could be called on or assigned some bullshit job at any time. In addition, as soon as we stepped aboard we were required to ditch our civilian clothes and put on our working uniforms, something the Airedales were not ordered to do.

Even with all this, I was having a ball and ignored the misery of living in the tank. I was in Alaska, on a ship, and one that was always going somewhere cool. And I was learning navigation, which was why I joined the Coast Guard in the first place. Working ATON on the Inside Passage was awesome. Whales, eagles and sea otters played around us while we worked the buoys, and at night the northern lights lit up the sky.

After a day of buoy tending, the *Clover* would pull into some nameless bay and drop the hook (anchor). Often we would take the ship's boat and go ashore exploring. Our captain was a very adventurous sort and was always eager to take the scenic route, even if it was off the beaten track. We took that ship places it never should have gone, but saw some amazing sights.

The SAR (Search and Rescue) calls were always exciting. In fact, exciting doesn't even begin to describe them. I figured I could only die once, so never was bothered by the fear that paralyzed some of the guys. I recognized that life on the *Clover* was definitely not for everyone though, and that leads me into this sea story.

My rate was quartermaster (QM) and we worked on the bridge, steering or "driving" the ship, or navigating. QM's were in the operations department or "Ops." Also in Ops were radiomen (RM's), radarmen (RD's) and electronic techs (ET's). These jobs tended to be a bit more technical or cerebral and attracted some smart guys that really had the wrong personality or emotional stability to be on a ship, especially the *Clover*. In other words, they were screwed.

One of the new QM's was Scott. Scott was a super nice guy and a great shipmate. He was well read and obviously very intelligent. We became good friends, even though as much as I was enjoying my suffering on the *Clover*, Scott positively hated it. He was miserable. Time after time he put in a request for a transfer. He didn't want out of the Coast Guard, he just wanted off the *Clover*. Time after time his request was denied.

**The John O'Connell Bridge connects Sitka,
on Baronof Island, with Japonski Island.**

One Saturday I was walking over the O'Connell Bridge, which spans the channel that separates Japonski Island from Sitka City proper. The O'Connell Bridge is a cable-stayed bridge over the Sitka Channel. It is 1255 feet in total length with a 450-foot main span. The roadway is 52 feet above the water. Japonski Island is mostly owned by the government and home to the Sitka Airport, the C.G. Air Station, various facilities run by the Bureau of Indian Affairs, and the CGC *Clover's* dock.

Our crew had recently completed cross-training qualifications as Emergency Medical Technicians, and as a community service we volunteered at the local fire hall for ambulance duty. I was heading to the fire hall to begin my volunteer shift.

I met Scott on the middle of the bridge. He was heading back toward the ship from town and carrying a large backpack, a common thing for the Coasties, usually full of Ranier or Olympia beer. We chatted for a minute and Scott asked me if I was going to be on the ambulance squad that day. I told him I was and had better get moving. He smiled and said, "Something's going to happen today and you're gonna love it." *Hmmm...cryptic.*

"OK, Scott, see ya later," I said and off I went.

I had no sooner arrived at the fire hall and checked in when the alarm went off. The dispatcher called into the ready room, "There's a guy on the bridge and he says he's going to jump. Get over there!" *Uh oh.* I had a weird feeling about this being linked together with Scott's mysterious message.

Tony and I got in the ambulance and got up on the bridge. The police were already there and had it closed off. There were three officers looking over the bridge rail, talking to somebody. One turned and said, "There's a guy down there tied to a bag of rocks and he says he's gonna jump if he doesn't get a transfer off the *Clover*."

I looked over the rail and there on one of the bridge abutments, about 15 feet down, was Scott, perched like a gargoyle on the edge.

"Hey, Scott," I called down. "Whatcha doin'?"

He looked up and yelled, "I can't take it anymore!"

"Scott, take it easy. Can I come down?" Then I whispered to the cops, "I'm on the *Clover*, I know him, let me talk to him."

Scott called back, "OK, Lonnie, but just you. Anybody else and I jump!"

I climbed down and sat on the cement alongside him. "Damn, Scott, it can't be this bad. That water is freakin' freezing, and the tide's coming in fast. Jump now and even with the rocks you'll be on your way to Japan."

"Relax man, I'm not gonna jump," he confided. "This is what we call 'street theater' back in New York City. You wanna help me sell it? Oh, by the way, want some beef jerky?"

"You know I will Scott, and sure, gimme a piece of that jerky."

"This might take a while," he warns.

"I got all day," I reply while munching away.

The cops yell down, "What's he say?"

"Like he said, he wants off the *Clover*. You better call Commander Jackson."

The *Clover* skipper shows up and boy is he ever pissed. Scott's making him look bad. He leans over the rail and starts screaming at Scott until the cops back him off. Scott stands up suddenly, smirking at the gasps this provokes from up above.

"I don't wanna talk to him," he says. "I want Captain Smathers from the air station."

"Ooo, smart move Scott," I say. "Smathers outranks Jackson. This will put them on the spot for sure."

A couple hours have passed and we're running low on jerky. Captain Smathers arrives. He's a pretty good guy and a square shooter. He starts talking to Scott sympathetically.

"I talked to District son, and you are officially transferred off the *Clover*. You work for me at the air station now. I guarantee that, now come on up."

"Is this on the level, Cap?" I ask Smathers. "You know he's not crazy for wanting off the *Clover*."

"No argument there," he replies. "But it's a done deal, so bring him up."

Scott turns to me and says, "Thanks, Brother," and with a wink lets the pack full of rocks go. It hits the water with a splash and scares the crap out of everybody on the bridge. They had all turned away thinking it was over. We both laughed. That was a cool way to wrap it up.

We climbed back up and Captain Smathers gives Scott a big hug. Off they go to the air station and I'm sure some type of a psych exam. But like I said, it wouldn't be crazy to want out of the tank.

Everybody on the bridge is shaking my hand and telling me I did a super job talking Scott out of jumping. *Ha ha...not hardly,* but I had to play it out. Scott had played the whole bunch of them and had an amusing day in the process. I enjoyed helping him con the Coast Guard too. They should have just given him the transfer when he asked.

I got back to the ship and our skipper had calmed down. He throws an arm around my shoulder, "Good work out there today, Calloway, really nice job."

"It was nothing, Cap. My shipmate needed help and I happened to be there." I was suitably modest. Scott needed help all right, just not the kind Cap thought.

Damn, I thought, *when the rest of the crew hears how Scott got out of the tank, they'll be jumping off that bridge like lemmings.*

20

Great Balls of Fire

Like most shipboard jobs, working on a tugboat is usually days of boredom punctuated by moments of sheer terror. It's those moments, and knowing they are coming, that keep you on your toes.

Cruising up the Inside Passage on the tugboat, *Zephyr*, daily life onboard quickly settles into a routine. Towing the huge freight barge *Mercury*, the *Zephyr* was enroute to Kodiak with a layover in Sitka and a brief stop in Cordova.

The *Mercury* was loaded "full and down," meaning she was fully loaded and down to her proscribed draft marks. She couldn't hold another case of whiskey. There was AvGas in her tanks below deck bound for the Coast Guard base on Kodiak.

Shipping containers, stacked three-high on the deck, carried everything from machine parts and automobiles to hemorrhoid cream. On this trip, the huge beams crossing on top of the containers supported fishing boats bound for Bristol Bay, new trucks for the North Slope, and a brand new snowplow for the City of Cordova. Also riding on top of the stack was a 30-foot motor home belonging to a chief petty officer in the Coast Guard, who was being transferred to Base Kodiak.

Loading the barge and lashing everything down tight.

Towing along behind the *Zephyr*, the *Mercury* was behaving. She was trimmed properly and tracking true behind the tug. Coming up the twists and turns of the Inside Passage, the towline was reeled in, keeping the barge closer to the tug ("up short" or "at short stay") and easier to control. When the tow reached open ocean, the line was spooled out almost a quarter mile ("on the string") and adjusted so both tug and barge were riding up the faces of the waves at the same time. Called being "in step," this reduced shock and excess drag on the towline.

A concern that was always in the back of tug crews' minds was the fact that the barge *was actually back there*, connected to the boat. If the tug had engine problems or suddenly hit something and stopped, the barge was barreling straight for them. Rolling along at ocean speed, the barge was a mindless mass as big as a school. The weight of the tow cable sinking deeper into the water also added to the inertia drawing barge and tug together.

There were two worst case scenarios. First, the barge could run over the tug, crushing her below the surface. Second, the barge could overtake and pass the tug, the attached towline rolling her over sideways and sinking her. This was called "girding" and was to be avoided at all costs.

Whenever the towline was adjusted, a rag was tied to it over a marked spot on deck so it would be easy to see if the towline was slipping. The guys checked it constantly. They'd check, re-check and then check again. Hour after hour, day after day, on-watch for four hours and off-watch for eight. There were always two men on watch: the captain or mate were in the wheelhouse, and a deckhand or engineer were below and making rounds of the boat.

In the engine room there were a dozen things to be checked and logged every hour. In the back of the engine room, just behind the engine, was a big easy chair mounted on a solid frame. Although it was ungodly loud down there, with the proper ear protection it was bearable. Most of the deckhands stayed in that chair between rounds. This was convenient for keeping an eye on the engine, and because it was as low in the boat as you could get, the ride was better. If you pulled out the third drawer in the file cabinet, you could put your feet up.

After stops in Sitka and Cordova, the *Zephyr* was hugging the north coast of the Gulf of Alaska, "beachcombing" her way around to Kodiak. Everything had been running smooth so far on the trip. I'd just finished checking the oil and logging all the gauges, and was kicked back in the easy chair daydreaming about vacation and palm trees. The easy rocking of the boat together with the vibration and muted thunder of the engine had me feeling sleepy.

With no warning, BOOOM! There's a loud explosion and a big fireball blows out the side of the engine, six feet in front of my chair. It takes a two-foot square steel inspection plate with it and crisps my eyebrows. Immediately the engine starts making a sick noise and I can feel us slowing down. Portside of the engine's on fire, and flames are blocking my exit on that side. Luckily there were ladders on both sides of the engine so I was out of there like a scalded dog, damn near peeing my pants.

Cap hits the kill switch and stops the engine, and I close off the fuel line. He fires off the CO_2 system in the engine room and that puts out the fire, which is good news. We might sink but we won't burn.

Relieved to escape the fire, I happen to glance back behind the tug. *Holy crap!* I forgot about our barge! I see the *Mercury* still trucking along and closing fast. All the guys were awake now and piling out the door. And all are now staring back in horror at the approaching disaster.

We start pulling survival suits on as fast as we can. Captain gets on the radio and puts out a call saying if he doesn't call again in 15 minutes, it means we're down and, *Send help!* Luckily it was still daylight but getting on toward evening. The weather was nice with a light wind and seas were fairly calm.

I'm thinking: Oooohh…this is really bad, but it still could have occurred at a worse time and place, like out in the middle of the Gulf of Alaska at night in a storm. I mean, at least we'll die within sight of land! I'm a glass-half-full kind of guy.

Clustered on the stern in our "Gumby suits," we watched, mesmerized, as the barge keeps rolling in on us. We could see every weld and rust streak on her bow and, to me, she looked mean. We were watching for a hint as to which side she would hit so we could jump over the opposite rail.

On she came, closer by the second, but gradually slowing down. As she came up behind us, there was a brief gust of wind. It was just enough to move the tug and turn the *Mercury's* bow. She slid up alongside us and stopped, almost touching. There was a big whoosh as we all let out the breath we'd been holding.

Cap ran up to the wheelhouse to cancel the mayday call and arrange a tow. We stripped off our survival suits and reeled in all the towline we could. We threw a few lines on the barge to hold her, and then just drifted around until help showed up.

A tug came out of Homer and towed our whole show into Kachemak Bay. We couldn't take the barge into town, so we planned to tie it off to a mooring buoy located in a cove on the far side of the bay. But we couldn't just leave it there, because…pirates. And that's no shit.

A barge-load of goodies is like a floating Walmart. There are containers full of every kind of booze there is, plus groceries, computers and chainsaws. You name it, we had it. Leaving a barge-load of stuff out in the boonies unattended was just asking for the locals to come out of the tree-line in their skiffs and pick it clean. Just like the old-time "wreckers."

This was an activity as old as time. Towing up the inside route we passed isolated, off-the-grid villages. As we went by, the locals would jump in their skiffs and chase the barge. It was easy to get on, since there are footholds cut in each side. It was illegal for us to have personnel riding the barge underway and they all knew it. The pirates would climb on the barge, break into a container, and start lowering booty to their associates in the boat. We never knew exactly when they were there. Even "up short" behind the tug, the barge was still a good distance back. We couldn't see over the container stacks at anything happening on its stern anyway.

Native settlements like this one—part of the village of False Pass—dot the windswept bays of the Aleutian Islands chain.

Because of this, the booze containers and the expensive, important stuff were buried in the stack. The outer row of containers was lashed down with the door facing in, and butted up against the next row. The only containers left on the outside of the stack had toilet paper, diapers, paper towels and things like that. The thinking was: We know they're going to get on, so let 'em waste time stealing big, bulky, cheap paper stuff. By the time they get through with that we'll be past and gone. It was a cost of doing business. We also kind of thought those folks could really use that stuff, and saw it as paying a toll. No hard feelings. We wouldn't want to live out there.

But leaving a nice shiny load of prime stuff out in the wilds by itself was just asking for it. Cap tells me and Randy, the other deckhand, "You guys have to stay with the barge. We'll be back to get you as soon as we can." Randy and

I were stoked about this. We get to hang out on the barge and skate, while the rest of the crew has to help repair the engine. *Sucks to be them!*

Heavy chain lashings hope to be pirate-proof.

The cook makes us up a bag with all kinds of food: sandwiches, sodas, cheese, chips…we were gonna have a picnic. Cap said to pop a box (container) and make a nest. We already had a *much* better plan. The last thing he did was hand me a spotlight and a pistol. "Don't shoot anybody unless you have to," were his parting words of wisdom.

The tug wasn't even out of sight before we were climbing into that beautiful motor home up on top. *Wow, was this ever sweet.* The keys were in it and the gas tank was full, so we had heat and music. We even had a nice place to sleep. Plus the refrigerator was full of cold beer. That Coast Guard chief really had it set up nice. And the view out the windshield was fantastic.

All we had to do was walk around and be visible every now and then. At night, we'd flash the spotlight around every so often. Word quickly spread through the jungle telegraph that the barge was manned, so the local pirates left us alone. I was really glad I didn't have to shoot a local minister or maybe the town mayor out for a little backwoods plunder.

The tug finally got fixed, and a few days later it came by to pick us up and grab the barge. We'd had a blast on "pirate patrol" and were sad to check out of our four-star hotel and return to our dismal racks on the *Zephyr*.

The rest of the trip was thankfully uneventful. My knees still got weak realizing that just a few minutes before the explosion, I had been standing right in front of that inspection plate taking readings. There is an old saying that goes, "God watches out for fools and sailors." I qualified on both counts so was doubly grateful for the protection.

Watching the longshoremen unload the barge in Kodiak, Randy and I were standing on the dock. A guy comes up and stops beside us. He points at the motor home being lowered off the barge with a crane. "That's my rig," he says proudly. "Glad she made it."

"It's a nice one, Chief," Randy says, and gives me a wink. We hoped he didn't miss his beer.

21

Feeding Time at the Zoo

If a guy isn't bat-shit nuts when he first sets foot on a Merchant Marine ship of any kind, just give him time. The isolation and the stress alone would do most people in, but living in close quarters for months at a time with people you would cross the street to avoid really takes a toll. Add to this the constant noise of a working vessel, the low roar of the blowers, the throb of the diesels, and the general banging and clanging of all the equipment flogging around as the boat rocks and rolls, often violently. Imagine tipping your house on its side and shaking it every thirty seconds or so. It's like that.

Plus you live with a terrible sleep schedule and the sure knowledge that it isn't if some horrible catastrophe is waiting to happen, it's *when*. It's only a matter of time before something important breaks, catches fire, or explodes. Probably sooner than later. You might very well wake up dead. *Sleep tight, Cupcake.*

When a guy has been on a boat for too long, he's said to be "ripe." It's time to get the hell off for a while. My personal cue was when I found myself wanting to stab the engineer in the throat with a fork for the way he buttered his bread. You would have thought the guy was painting the Mona Lisa. Back and forth with the knife, back and forth...squinting at it critically...then back and forth some more. *I couldn't look away!* It was like watching ping pong.

"Jesus Christ, Andy, just eat the goddamn sandwich!"

My psychosis was only a symptom, not a disease. It was cured by getting off the boat for a time. I worked with many guys over the years that could be classified as certifiable loonies though. You can't fix that kind of insanity. You just transfer them to another boat.

Take Ted and Mike, for example. These two were brothers who both worked for an Alaskan tug and barge as cooks. As cooks go, they were pretty decent, but after the meals were served, crazy came out to play.

My first trip as deckhand on the tug *Zephyr* was on a winter run across the Gulf of Alaska to Kodiak with a freight/fuel barge in tow. Ted made a good supper: mac and cheese, green beans, and a bunch of other assorted side dishes.

During my evening watch I went down to the galley to grab a snack, but found nothing. There was nothing in the reefer and nothing on the tables. *What the hell?* I knew there were a ton of leftovers. About that time, the mate came in. "Hey Jack, I can't find the mac and cheese."

"That's because Ted hides everything like a freakin' squirrel," he said laughing. "Look around like you're huntin' Easter eggs." So I start looking high and low, opening drawers and cupboards. Here are the beans, up with the breakfast cereal. The bread is in the lifejacket box. The mac and cheese is under the stove with the cookie sheets. Everything is still in the pots it was cooked in.

Jack chuckled, "Old Ted's been doing this for years. Don't worry, you'll learn his favorite hiding spots." I eventually did. When it seemed normal, I knew it was time to get off.

Mike was another story entirely. Dubbed the "Strange Ranger," he was a Vietnam vet more than half a bubble off plumb. Like his brother, he was a good cook. No complaints there. But Mike had a disturbing hobby. He liked to make bombs. They were mainly for use in his rabid vendetta against the seagulls that followed the boat. Mike was convinced they personally shit on him when he was trying to fish. Telling him not to stand by the garbage cans went right over his head.

Down in the forepeak of the tug he had his little workshop. He would blow up a small balloon, about the size of a softball, then coat it in Bondo car putty to make a shell. When it was dry, he would coat it in glue and roll it around on a pan full of BB's. When that dried, he'd repeat the process a couple more times. He called it a "tugboat claymore."

Next he would fill the Bondo shell with black powder and stick in a waterproof fuse. Then he would bake a huge round loaf of bread, hollow it out, and lovingly pack his baby inside. The hatch to the forepeak was in the galley, and BANG! …the lid would fly open and Mike would come up, hair all sticking up and looking like a mad professor. He'd have smudges of gunpowder on his face, grinning like an idiot and cradling his latest creation.

"Anybody want some toast?" he would croon. "It's time for *toast*." He would go on humming to himself: "Toast toast toast…"

Back he would walk to the stern of the tug, the whole crew following him. We kind of did want some "toast," or at least to see something toasted. We were all pretty bored. Opening a bag of garbage, Mike chummed it overboard until a good sized flock of seagulls had gathered.

Lighting the fuse, he set the loaf bomb adrift. Back it floated until, with a gut thumping WHUUUMP, it detonated and vaporized any birds unlucky enough to still be in range. Bear in mind, we're towing a huge barge loaded with jet fuel and it's behind us "on the string," a bit less than a quarter mile back.

One time, the fuse was a little too long and his bomb almost detonated under the bow of the barge. The captain got pissed.

"Goddammit Mike, cut those fucking fuses shorter next time."

Toast!

22

Ripe as a Couple Melons

Continuing with the theme of being on the boat too long and being "ripe," I have to share this incident report I received when I was first mate on a large Great Lakes freighter. I received many such reports over the years, but this one is my all-time absolute favorite. It never fails to crack me up.

Both these guys were good people. They were just strung way too tight after being on the boat way too long. Normally, fights on a ship result in both parties being fired. However, coming up through the deck like I did, I was aware that these blow-ups didn't always mean guys hated each other, and I really didn't want to lose two good men.

Gary, the MA (mate's assistant, or wheelsman) was having a problem with Kirk, the steward (or cook). They were both being dickwads. Things obviously escalated out of all bounds of reason, and Kirk submitted this report.

To: 1st Mate

On board the M/V ********** at approx. 1635 hours, Wheelsman Gary ***** came into the galley and asked me for medium well sirloin of beef. I stated I didn't have it because of the oven kicking on and off. If he could do better than come back and do it. Wheelsman Gary ***** walked down the passageway to the recreation room stating "Fuck you, Fuck you, you fucking bean burner." I finished slicing the extra beef and walked to the rec room stating to Wheelsman Gary ***** if he wants to keep saying "fuck you" to me, then say it face to face like a man.

At that time he stood up and started punching me in the head saying "is this man enough for you"? I stated, "you have to get off me, at which time he punched me twice more then stopped. I turned and walked back to the galley with Wheelsman Gary **** behind me. At that time he said to me "Asshole, little girl, fuck you." I said to him, stop swearing at me, I'm not swearing at you.

At no time did I swear at Wheelsman Gary **** or hit him. We were both yelling at a higher level than normal, saying let's take this to the Captain. I said, no, not now, after the evening meal.

Kirk ********* (Steward)

Witnesses:
Bos'n
Chief Engineer
2nd Cook

I pulled both knuckleheads into my office and lowered the boom on them. I told them to "cut the shit, shake hands, and get back to work." I also told them, "If either one of you idiots bothers the captain with this junior-high crap, I will personally pound both of you. Now get outta here."

After they slunk out the door, I still about blew an onion laughing at the incident report.

Back in my bell bottom days, past ripe after 150 days on board, impatiently waiting for the supply boat, *Ojibway*, to come pick me up.

Appendix

Curious to learn a little more about working aboard a ship? For those who aren't Boat-nerds or already working on a boat or ship, you may find it interesting to get more of a taste of what it takes to move people and products across large bodies of water.

In 1936, the Propeller Club of the United States began the Adopt-A-Ship program. It was initiated as a way to teach kids about the "staunch character and dignity of the men and woman of the American Merchant Marine." The term Merchant Marine encompasses fleets of ocean and coastal vessels along with those on navigable rivers, lakes, bays and sounds, as well as harbor craft.

The idea was to exchange e-mails with the class and be sort of a sea-going pen pal. But before I climbed aboard the M/V *Buffalo* in September of 2002 I had never heard of the Adopt A-Ship program.

As a relief officer out of the Union Hall, I was signed aboard as third mate. On my first bridge watch, the captain showed me an e-mail. It was from the office, directing him to ask for volunteers to participate in a new company PR program pairing vessel crewmembers with an elementary school class somewhere in the country.

Imagine my surprise when he informed me that I had just "volunteered" for Adopt-A-Ship. *Lucky me!* I didn't really mind though. There are often long watches with not much to do and I thought this might help pass the time.

A few days later, the *Buffalo* was officially adopted by a class of fifth graders at the Pinehurst School in Salisbury, Maryland. From the start, it was a lot of fun. The kids asked great questions and seemed really interested in the travels of "their" iron ore freighter. I had a ball thinking back to other ships and shipmates and remembering stories to share with our class.

My watch partners got into it as well, eventually reading over my shoulder and giving me technical advice. They were constantly asking me to mention them in the next e-mail.

Photo courtesy of Roger LeLievre.

Great Lakes freighters like the *Buffalo* can carry the same amount of cargo as roughly 500 semitrailers, but use less than one-tenth the amount of fuel.

Each letter started out by telling the class our ship coordinates so the kids could track our movement on a chart we'd mailed them. I would also fill them in on the details of what materials we were now hauling and where we were heading. To keep things moving along, I will pare this part down a bit and take out redundant stories (yes, I told them much tamer versions). While perhaps more sweet than salty, many folks over the years have enjoyed reading through these letters, and I hope you do too. I sure enjoyed writing them.

By the way, you may notice the use of "Lonnie" in these e-mails instead of "Lon." On ships we use handheld radios to communicate while loading and unloading. It's always hard to hear and when there are crew members on deck named Ron, Don, Jon, Con and Lon, everybody has to keep asking "*Who are you calling?*" Going by "Lonnie" on the boats just made communication a whole lot more efficient.

Finally, I'll add that the reason I have these letters now is that every time I got a message from the kids, I copied it and sent it to my mom. She was delighted with them and waited by the mailbox for the next one. After she passed, I found these in her desk. So, *Thanks Mom!!*

The Great Lakes straddle the border between
Canada and the United States.

Hello Shipmates,

Good morning from the *Buffalo*! My name is Lonnie Calloway, and I will
be talking to you about life on the Great Lakes. I am the third mate on board.
My job is to stand a watch in the pilot house (also called the wheelhouse or the
ship's bridge). This is where we navigate and steer the ship. We stand watch four
hours on duty, and then we are off duty for eight hours. We do this around the
clock as long as we are on board.

Right now we are northbound in Lake Huron. We are carrying a cargo of
gypsum, which is a form of stone used to make plasterboard (or drywall). We
are bound for Waukegan, Illinois, so must travel up Lake Huron, around the
top of Michigan, through the Straits of Mackinac, and down Lake Michigan
almost to Chicago.

Fall is coming so the weather is cooling off. It is very windy out here today,
with west winds blowing almost thirty miles an hour. The *Buffalo* is a big ship so
even though the waves are getting bigger, we ride pretty well. We have a crew
of 24 on here, and they come from all over the country. I always enjoy the interesting people I meet as I work in this industry.

I live in Northern Michigan in a town called Indian River. I work all over
the Lakes and both coasts of the U.S. on all kinds of ships. Right now I am
working for American Steamship Company for another officer that is on vacation. I have been doing this for 28 years and have worked on over 75 different

ships! I love being a mariner and have had many great adventures.

I'm looking forward to sharing some of my stories with you over the next few weeks. First off, we will learn to tell time like a sailor. Ships run on military time or the 24-hour clock. There is no A.M. or P.M. The day starts at midnight, written 0000. One in the morning is written as 0100, pronounced "oh-one-hundred." Fifteen after three in the morning is 0315 or "oh-three-fifteen." Pretty easy so far. Continue like that until noon, then it gets tricky!

Since there are 24 hours in the day, the first 12 are numbered one through twelve. One in the afternoon is 1300 or "thirteen hundred," Two is 1400 or Fourteen hundred and so on. Midnight can be 2400 or 0000, and the day starts again. See if you can figure out what seven-fifteen in the evening would be and let me know.

Send me some questions and I will try to answer them. I will also share some pictures with you as we go along.

Until then, Smooth sailing…Lonnie

The *American Spirit* taking heavy spray on Lake Michigan.

Ahoy, Shipmates!

Good evening from the *Buffalo*. We've covered a lot of water since I wrote last and just finished loading limestone for a port in the St. Clair River called Marine City. It takes about 10 hours to load the *Buffalo* and it can carry around

22,000 tons. That's a big pile! The ship is a self-unloader, meaning it can unload without dockside assistance.

The cargo holds are shaped kind of like an egg carton, with small trap doors at the bottom of each compartment. A conveyor belt runs underneath the holds, and that connects to another belt that goes up to the deck. When we unload, the belt starts up and crew members, called conveyormen and gatemen, open the trap doors in a certain order and let the cargo fall on the moving belt. We have a long boom (steel structure to support a belt) on deck that swings over the side and extends over the dock. This way we can move the product out of the holds, up on deck, and off the ship. It's very efficient, unloading the whole ship in around four or five hours.

You had some good questions, and I'll try to answer a few. We do have a lot of spare time, and you can't sleep all the time, so if you can't find ways to entertain yourself you might not want to be a sailor! I read a lot, mostly novels, but some textbooks as we are always studying to upgrade our licenses. We also have satellite TV in our rooms.

Most ships have an extensive video library so you can watch movies. I take a lot of pictures and write letters to my friends. A lot of crewmembers go for walks, as the ship is 617 feet long. That is a little longer than two whole football fields laid end to end. In the summer the crew calls the deck "steel beach" and lay out in the sun. Working 4 hours on and 8 hours off gets to be a routine and time passes pretty fast.

The letters M/V stand for Motor Vessel and are part of the ships official designation. In the old days, more ships were designated "S.S." and that stood for steamship. Some other designations are S/V for sailing vessel, R/V for research vessel and P/V for pleasure craft, or small boats. Can you guess what F/V stands for?

Normally, the normal crew rotation is 60 days on and 30 days off. It hardly ever works out that way, however. The Coast Guard requires mariners to have so many different qualifications these days that sometimes finding reliefs can be difficult. The longest I ever stayed on a ship without going home was 6 months. I was pretty young then and just starting out so I didn't want to get off. I sure couldn't do that kind of time anymore!

Well, my watch is drawing to a close and I have to go do some ship work: put a position down on the chart and sign all the logbooks. I'll continue *this* logbook in a couple days. Until then, Fair Winds…Lonnie

P.S. You were correct in figuring seven fifteen was 1915. Good work!

Steel Beach on a snotty day.

Good Evening Shipmates,

We are northbound ("upbound") in Lake Huron. It's 2114 and I am part-way through the evening watch. This is an "open lake" watch, meaning we are out of the rivers and on a straight course up the lake. It's a little more laid back than restricted water watches, but of course we still have to stay on our toes. Since I do have a little time, I wanted to finish answering your questions and tell you a bit more about sailing.

Our route to Waukegan last week was 460 miles one way. Our office is sending you a chart of the Great Lakes and it has a distance scale on it. You will be able to calculate our mileage and I can see how close you get. When you get the chart (maps are to look at, charts are to work on) you may wish to mark our regular ports of call.

There are three departments on most ships: deck, engine, and stewards (cooks). We have three cooks on board and they serve three meals a day. Traditionally, Saturday night is steak night on Great Lakes ships and that's always great!

The captain is in overall charge of the ship but also heads up the deck department. He has three officers under him, one on each watch. Also on each deck watch is a wheelsman (or helmsman) and another sailor called an able sea-

141

man. I'm really lucky to have a very competent wheelsman, named Bob, on my watch. He really knows his business and helps me a lot.

The able seaman on my watch is Manny, and he is also the ship's boatswain (pronounced bosun and traditionally spelled bos'n). He is the guy that supervises the deckhands and knows everything about operating the ship's deck gear. Without professional seamen like these, it would be difficult for the ship to operate.

With the boat still moving, a bos'n used a "landing boom" to put deckhands on the dock to handle tie-up lines. After we got on the wooden seat, the bos'n swung the boom arm over the side and ZIP...down you go—hopefully not into the lake!

While there are no women on board at this time, that is only a coincidence. These jobs are open to women and there are quite a few women working the Lakes in every job from cook to captain.

One point of interest, today we stopped at the gas station, better known as the fuel dock. The *Buffalo* burns a lot of fuel so it takes a while to gas up. Today we took on 75,000 gallons of diesel fuel. It took a little over an hour as the fuel dock can pump 1000 gallons a minute.

When you get your chart, I will be sending you our position in latitude and longitude. Latitude is always written first and is measured north or south of the equator. It is the scale up the sides of the chart and can be remembered by thinking of a ladder. Longitude is written second and is measured either east or west of Greenwich, England. On a chart the scale is across the bottom and top. For instance our position right now would be written Pos: 43 degrees 45 minutes North/ 82 degrees 31 minutes West. Each degree has 60 minutes, so you see minutes can be used to measure distance as well as time.

I also wanted to give you a quick lesson in ship terms so you don't sound like "land-lubbers." First, the front of the ship is the "bow," and the back of the ship is the "stern." Stairways are "ladders," doors are "hatches," and windows are "ports." When walking toward the bow, you are going "forward," and going toward the stern you are going "aft." Of course there are many more but we are just getting started.

Until next time, Fair Winds...Lonnie

As we enter the Welland Canal, which uses eight locks to bypass Niagara Falls, I was already calculating the overtime.

Good Evening Shipmates,

Time is 2215, and our position is 42 degrees 33 minutes N / 86 degrees 59 minutes W. The *Buffalo* is downbound in Lake Michigan with 21,805 tons of limestone aboard. Bob and I are having an easy watch tonight. We will be steering the same course for our whole watch.

To understand how we navigate you need to know that a circle is divided into 360 degrees. Imagine the ship is at the center. Whichever direction we want to go can be assigned a three digit number, north being 000 degrees, east being 090 degrees, south being 180 degrees, and west being 270 degrees. Right now we are steering 187 degrees which is just a few degrees past south.

We determine our position by several methods. We have a very sophisticated radar set that is computerized and interfaced with a machine called a chart plotter. This shows our motion across a color chart in our real position. We can also use the radar to tell how far we are from a specific point of land we are going past. When this distance is marked on the chart we can tell where we are.

The most accurate tool we have is called GPS. A receiver picks up a signal from a satellite and converts it to a position. (A minimum of three satellites are needed to get a good fix, but we may be receiving data from as many as nine at any given time.)

Another ship coming shows up on the radar screen as a dot of light. The radar gives us a readout on its course, speed, distance away, and most important, its CPA. This stands for "closest point of approach" and lets us know if we need to alter course to stay clear and avoid a collision.

This is all kind of technical stuff, but it's important to know that ships are not just driving around aimlessly, but are on very specific tracks at all times.

I'll lighten things up for a while and tell you some more nautical terms. Hallways are "passageways," beds are "bunks," walls are "bulkheads" and bathrooms are called "heads."

Bob is making some fresh coffee so I will close for now. Fair Winds... Lonnie

Good Morning Shipmates,

Thank you for the nice letter. Your guesses about the meaning of F/V— freight vessel, fast vessel, fuel vessel—were very good. It actually stands for "fishing vessel." That was a hard one!

I lived and worked in Alaska for many years and worked for a while on the F/V *Donna Lee*. We fished for halibut. The biggest one we ever caught weighed 350 pounds and was 9 feet long!

Since the ships are usually running into December we do have to spend many holidays on board. Our union contracts give us more money, called "Holiday Pay," on special days. The cooks go all out and in addition to turkey and ham, we usually have lobster. We normally have a wide range of choices of things to eat (not just steak). There is always a salad bar. We eat about like we would at home, we just have someone else cooking for us.

One of the most important things on board is getting mail. We have a very unique way to do this. There is a little boat in the Detroit River called the *J.W. Wescott II* that has been delivering mail to passing ships since 1874. It is the only boat in the country with its own zip code. We call about an hour away and tell them we are coming, then when we get close they come charging out and come alongside as we keep moving down the river. We lower a pail in a line and they put our mail, newspapers and such in the bucket, then we pull it up and give the mail boat a salute on our whistle (one long blast and two shorts means "hi," "bye," or "thanks, see ya next time"). Sometimes they bring crew members to the ship and they climb up a ladder.

The mailboat in Detroit has its own zip code. It comes alongside the ship and the crew lowers a bag or a bucket. The mail goes down, the mail comes up, then away they go.

Sailors have a lot of time on their hands and one way we'd entertain ourselves was with elaborate practical jokes. So when you are a young new guy— also called a "green" hand—you really have to watch out! One of the old favorites was the "mail buoy" watch.

Here's how it worked: Somebody would casually mention to the victim that we'd be going by the mail buoy soon and to get any letters he wanted to send ready. It would be explained that the U.S. Post Office maintained a special buoy out in the lake, where our mail was dropped. This buoy was kind of hard to see so we usually had to set up a buoy watch.

After lunch, or some time when everybody was up, the mate, or bos'n would call down and tell the new guy that we were getting close and to gear up, go forward, and sing out when he spotted the buoy.

The poor guy would be rigged out in hard hat, safety glasses, lifejacket, binoculars, and armed with a net and boathook. The crew would see how long it took for him to figure out there was no such thing as a mail buoy. Some guys would catch on quick and others would stay up there for hours.

We are upbound heading for Port Inland. The remains of Hurricane Lilli are causing some bad weather on the Lakes. We were anchored yesterday for a while until the wind went down. It was blowing over 50 miles an hour in some spots! Even a big ship like the *Buffalo* starts bouncing around pretty good in high wind and big waves. It was kind of exciting. I have been in some terrible storms in my career at sea and will tell you about them another time.

Until next time, Smooth Sailing…Lonnie

As captain of a ferry to Mackinac Island, I watched the crew loading Belgian horses for the upcoming tourist season.

Good Morning Shipmates,

It's 0846, and the *Buffalo* is downbound in Lake Michigan. Today we are carrying what is called a split load of limestone. That means we have different kinds of stone in different holds, and will be stopping in two ports to unload.

Writing to you reminds me of when my daughter was in fifth grade. Right now she is a senior at Western Michigan University, in Kalamazoo, Michigan. When she was your age we lived in Southeast Alaska in a town called Sitka. I worked as a helmsman for the Alaska Marine Highway, a ferry system designed to connect all the island communities of S.E. Alaska with each other and with the lower 48 (the rest of the country).

Jessica loved to take trips with me, especially on the M/V *Columbia*, the biggest ship in the fleet and the one that ran down to Seattle. It was 418 feet long and carried 1000 passengers and 180 cars. She learned to steer the ship and got pretty good at it. We had to put a plastic milk case in front of the wheel for her to stand on so she could see out the window!

A few more nautical terms: the left side of the ship is the "port" side and the right is the "starboard" side (usually written "stbd"). A rope is only called "rope" when it is still on the reel it came on. Once it has been cut to a length for a specific purpose it is called a "line." Here's a funny one: drinking fountains on ships are called "scuttlebutts." Shipboard rumors are also called "scuttlebutt" as in "what's the latest scuttlebutt?" I think that comes from the old days when sailors would gather around the water barrel and swap gossip.

Time to get back to work, so I will send this off.

Until next time, Fair Winds…Lonnie

Good Morning Shipmates,

0852 on a Friday morning. Eastbound approaching the Straits of Mackinac (pronounced "Mackinaw"). The stone quarry is really out in the sticks, in fact the loading crew has a tame family of foxes that live on the dock! They are so tame that they beg food from the ships that come in. There are four black ones and two red ones. They are very sleek and well fed, and it's funny to see them romping around on the dock!

Thank you for the letter! You had some good questions. Bob and I laughed when you asked for a picture of my room (on modern ships only the captain's room is called a "cabin"). All the rooms are nice on the *Buffalo*, each having a private bathroom and shower. The crew have two persons in a room. As an officer I have a room to myself, with a big double bed, a desk, refrigerator, reclining easy chair and a TV.

I live one deck down from the pilothouse on "C" deck, along with the captain and the other two mates. This is so we can get to the bridge quickly if we have to. I don't think a picture of my room would look very good as it usually looks like a bomb went off in it! I have equipment all over the place, rain gear, hard hats, gloves, radio, binoculars, etc., plus charts, work clothes and all kinds of stuff. At bedtime I just kick enough out of the way to make room for myself and fall in!

Sitting on a sea buoy to check its position on Sitka Sound.

Yes, I did have the "mail buoy" trick played on me when I was first starting out. I had heard about it already though so knew what to expect. I decided to play along and turn the trick around on the crew. They really thought they had a "greenie," I was so eager to go watch for the mail buoy! I let them gear me up with all the stuff and went forward to the lookout position. To make it look real, the mate even went to the crew mailbox and put everybody's outgoing mail in a bag for me. I was counting on this! As I went forward, I switched the real bag of mail for a bag full of old newspapers.

I put on a good show of looking for the buoy and the whole crew was laughing at me. After I had been up there for a while, I got on the radio and started yelling, "There it is!!! I see the mail buoy!!" Then I took the bag and threw it over the side, hollering, "I'm delivering the mail!" Well, the boys almost went nuts, thinking I threw all their mail overboard. You should have seen the faces! I laughed for a week!

**After checking the buoy position, we'd get hoisted off.
Best. Thrill. Ever!**

There are lots of tricks guys play on each other but I probably shouldn't tell too many of them! I don't want to get in trouble with your parents or your teacher! OK, OK, I'll tell you one more of the favorites but DON'T TRY THIS AT HOME. Guys like to sneak into the bathrooms and unscrew the shower heads. Then they put two or three lemon drops inside and screw it back on. When the victim takes a shower, the hot water melts the candy and coats the person with sugar water. When he dries off, he can't figure out why he is so sticky all over!

I told this one to Jessica one time and forgot about it. A few days later I took a shower and just didn't feel right afterward. All of a sudden the light in my head popped on and I checked my shower. Sure enough, there were the remains of two lemon drops inside the shower head! She thought she was so clever!

The *Buffalo* is named for Buffalo, N.Y., the city our company offices are located in. Very few American Great Lakes ships have cool names. Most are named for the chairmen of the board or other company executives. I prefer more romantic names for ships, as I think of them as beautiful things.

We will be in the rivers (St. Clair and Detroit Rivers) for about 10 hours tomorrow morning. These rivers connect Lake Huron and Lake Erie and are very challenging to navigate compared to open water sailing. I'll tell you more about that as we get closer.

Well, back to work for me. Until next time, Smooth Sailing…Lonnie

To "trim out" the load, the mate on watch goes down to the dock—
as limestone is thundering into the hold—and works to balance
the boat. When you need just a little more, you tell the loader to
"gimme a squirt." A squirt is a shot of 10 tons of product!

Good Morning Shipmates,

It's been a very busy few days and I haven't had much time to write to you.
After unloading our stone load in Ashtabula, Ohio, the *Buffalo* was sent to Lorain, Ohio for three shuttle loads up the river in Cleveland. We load iron ore in
Lorain, then it is a short two-hour run to the Cleveland harbor entrance. After
that the fun starts.

The captain has to slowly run the ship way up the Cuyahoga River to the
steel mill. It takes almost three hours and is quite a feat of seamanship. At times
there is only *15 feet* on either side of the ship to the bank. My job is to stand way
up on the bow of the ship with a radio and tell the captain how much room he
has up front or "over the head." Mick, the bos'n, does the same thing on the
stern of the ship.

I'll take a few minutes and tell you a little about loading the ship. The first thing you need to know is that a ship is rarely empty. A totally empty ship rides so high out of the water that the propeller is not very effective. Also, cooling water intakes don't function well and the ship is unstable in bad weather. So to keep the ship at a proper level, we use "ballast." Ballast is anything heavy a ship carries for weight in place of cargo. In the old days ships carried rocks or bricks to the loading port, then dumped them in exchange for cargo. Today, ships use water for ballast.

There are tanks beneath the cargo hold, the length of the ship, called "ballast tanks." As we load the ship we slowly pump the ballast water out at the same rate the cargo is coming in. We also have to carefully watch for "list," which is how much the ship tips from side to side. Adjusting the ballast and the load to keep the ship even is called "trimming" the ship.

As we near the end of the loading process, we watch to make sure that we end up even from side to side, and a little deeper aft than forward to make the ship cut through the water correctly. We also want to make sure the ballast water is all out so we are carrying the maximum weight in cargo.

It's hard to believe I have been on the *Buffalo* for a month already! I will be here for another three weeks, then home for a week, then back out. I will miss both Thanksgiving and Christmas at home but my family understands that this is my job and that's the way it goes. We always have a big celebration when I come home!

I have to do a few things so will end for now. Fair Winds…Lonnie

Good Morning Shipmates,

We hit some bad weather last night and really took a ride! After a few hours of walking on the walls ("bulkheads"), the captain changed course and anchored in Green Bay. We spent the night "riding the hook" and left at daybreak.

A little about the anchor. The *Buffalo* carries three 2-ton anchors, two forward and one aft. Each one is connected to 450 feet of chain. Anchor chain is divided up in 90 foot sections called "shots." Each link of chain is a foot long and weighs 80 pounds. Technically it isn't the anchor that holds a ship in place but the weight of the chain on the bottom! When we drop the anchor, or "hook," the mate and the bos'n go forward to the anchor room (called the "windlass" room for the big winch that raises the anchor).

The anchor must first be "cleared," that is released from the restraining tackle that keeps it from dropping itself in heavy seas. Then when the captain is ready, he will say on the radio something like, "let go the starboard anchor, three shots on deck." That means: release the brake and allow the anchor to drop. We let the chain run out until the third shot mark is just passing over the deck on its way over the side.

The box the chain is stowed in is the "chain locker," and the pipe that passes from the chain locker to the anchor is the "hawse pipe." (In sailor talk, a deck officer like myself that worked his way up from the deck gang to the pilothouse is said to have "come up through the hawse pipe.")

On the bridge of the *Buffalo*.

I said I would tell you a little more about the rivers we went through last week. To get from Lake Huron to Lake Erie it is necessary to travel through two rivers and across a small lake. The St. Clair River starts in Port Huron and runs south for 39 miles to lake St. Clair. In some places it is very narrow, and it always twists and turns. There is current, lots of other traffic, and sometimes fog. As pilots, we have to take a very difficult exam to qualify for a river license.

You have to draw the whole river from memory, including every light and buoy. You also have to know all the different courses both up and down. We start and end our turns using landmarks, so a wheel command might sound like this: Start easing her left, and steer on the shopping center."

Here are a couple navigation terms for you. A "fix" is a position you have marked on a chart. We usually just plot the lat/long from the GPS receiver, but I throw in a radar range from the beach to check it. A "route" is the combination of different courses, or "legs," that take the ship from its starting point to the destination. A "waypoint" is the end of one course leg and the start of another, so a route is like connecting the dots, or connecting a series of waypoints until we get where we want to go.

Time to go back to work, so until next time, Fair Winds...Lonnie

It was clear early on that I possessed many of
the skills needed to become a good sailor.

Good Evening Shipmates,

Right now we are in Stoneport, a loading facility near Alpena, Michigan. We are taking on a partial load of limestone here, then going north to Drummond Island to finish the load. We often take different grades (sizes) of stone in different cargo holds, but for this load we are taking different kinds of stone from two quarries. Loads like this are called "shake and bakes."

This means we have an equal amount of two kinds of stone on board, in this case 9700 tons of each. When we unload, instead of unloading each kind in a separate pile, we open two different cargo holds and let the stone mix on the belt as it goes off the ship. This is used in the steel-making process. It's kind of a pain to load it like this, but that's what the customer wants.

You had a bunch of great questions and I will get right to answering them. All of the lighthouses (except Crisp Point) are still in use. They are all automated so there are no keepers any more. Every light has characteristics that are different from other lights around it. These are marked on the chart by each light position. The charts we use to navigate are much more area-specific and are very detailed.

If there are light characteristics on your chart they might look something like this: "FL 1Os 78ft 17St m." That means the light is white (if it were green or red it would say FL G or FL R), it is 78 feet tall and can be seen from 17 statute miles away. It flashes once every 10 seconds. This way if a sailor was lost but had a chart or a "light list," he could tell where he was by the flash pattern of the light. Pretty neat!

Every person on board a ship, including the captain, has chores. These are divided up so everyone knows exactly what they are responsible for. For the lower ranks, there are "cleaning stations" that they are required to hit every day. The officers have more paperwork to do. I am responsible for keeping the ships log up to date. American Steamship Co. has a very complex logbook and it takes a lot of time to keep it current.

Each watch officer enters positions and weather observations on their own watch, but I have to enter all our cargo data, like tonnage loaded, what product, what holds it went in, tonnage per hold, times started and finished loading or unloading, and any delays. I also must keep track of fuel at the start and finish of each trip as well as miles traveled both empty and loaded. In addition to that I have to keep a load book that tells each port, cargo, and tonnage and keep a running tally of tonnage carried this season. So far this year, the *Buffalo* has moved 1,438,498 tons of cargo!

No, my dad wasn't a sailor. He was an air traffic controller. My mom was a school teacher, and in fact was my teacher as a sub in most lower grades and all year in 6th grade. We still tease my brother because the only time he ever got in trouble in school was when he got a spanking from our mom when he was in kindergarten! I have one brother and one sister, but I'm the only sailor. I always liked ships and used to draw them all the time when I was little.

I got seaman's papers right out of high school but couldn't find a job on a boat. I went to Michigan State University for three years and was studying to be a teacher myself when I got a temporary job on a ship. Well, that's all she wrote. I've been on ships ever since. I haven't had a job on the beach in 28 years!

Seasickness is kind of an occupational hazard. Most people get used to the "motion of the ocean" and it doesn't bother them, but some people never get over it. When it gets really rough, especially on small boats, it's hard not to feel a little off at first. I haven't been seasick for years but had a few moments in the Gulf of Alaska on a fishing boat I wasn't too thrilled with.

Sailors love it if somebody in the crew is seasick and they show them no mercy. Guys fire up big cigars around the poor victim or start telling stories of horrible things to eat. First time I got seasick, I was laying in my rack praying for death. The old timers came in and draped my wracked body with a flag.

I've been working as a captain on the Arnold Line Ferries for 10 years, mostly during the summer tourist season in Northern Michigan. Mackinac Island is a popular tourist destination with over a million visitors a year. Cars are outlawed so the only transportation is horses or bikes. The island was an important fur trading outpost in the 1700's and has a restored fort from that time.

There are three ferry boat companies and 25 ferries that serve the island. Jessica started working for Arnold Line when she was 15 and worked there for 4 summers. She worked as a deckhand on my boat a bunch of times. I told her "I have you, now! I'm the captain and you have to do whatever I say." She just laughed and said, "Dream on, Dad." We had a lot of fun working together!

We already learned to tell ship's time, now I will tell you about our alphabet. We talk on the radio a lot and sometimes reception is poor and it is hard to understand what is being said. When we need to spell words and to make it easier to understand, we use what is called the "phonetic alphabet." Each letter of the regular alphabet is assigned a word to use in place of it. It goes like this: Alpha, Bravo, Charlie, Delta, Echo, Foxtrot, Golf, Hotel, India, Juliet, Kilo, Lima, Mike, November, Oscar, Papa, Quebec, Romeo, Sierra, Tango, Uniform, Victor, Whiskey, X-Ray, Yankee, and Zulu. See what your name sounds like using this system.

Until next time, Smooth Sailing…Lonnie

Good Morning Shipmates,

We're westbound in Lake Erie. Weather is cold and rainy so deck work hasn't been too much fun, but we dress for it so it's not too bad.

The Lakes are pretty wide open, with lots of room but at a few places due to shoals, reefs, or islands the shipping lanes all come together in narrow spots called "choke points." We are on a straight course for our whole watch but the next watch has to navigate through a choke point called Pelee Pass. These can get crowded at times and very tense, especially at night or in the fog! See if you can find these other choke points: Grays Reef Pass, North Manitou Pass, Mackinac Bridge, Poe Reef Pass, Rock Island Pass and Round Island Pass.

There is one pass from Lake Michigan into Green Bay called "Portes Des Martes," which means "Death's Door." It is a nasty, rock-filled passage that is well named!

Sometimes the captain has us taking a "weather route," which means we run close to shore to stay out of the wind as much as possible. A route like this is called "beachcombing" since we are so far in from the normal shipping lanes.

On watch, piloting the 1000-footer *George A. Stinson* down the St. Marys River through a narrow, man-made ditch called the Rock Cut, with less than two feet of clearance underneath.

I'll tell you a little more about navigating in the rivers we travel. There are many buoys that mark safe channels but they can be moved by current or ice. Currents also greatly affect the ship, moving it one way or another (called being "set"). To give ship pilot's a better idea of their position in a channel, there are "range lights." These are special lights set up at each end of a channel to show the middle. They are either on shore or permanently constructed so as not to be affected by weather or currents.

Here's how they work. They are built in pairs, in line with the center of the channel. The rear one is taller and usually has a fixed light (one that is on steadily). The other one is lower and 200 yards or more in front with a light that flashes. They also have big orange boards attached to them called "dayboards" to see in daylight. The idea is to keep these markers lined up. If they are out of line, you can tell by which side the front range is off, and if you are left or right of the channel.

You're right, there are lots of funny names around the ships. Here are a few more unofficial names that are used in fun. Engineers are called "snipes" and pilots are called "navi-guessors." The engine room is called "the basement" and the pilot house is called the "brain-box."

The deck crew and the engine room crew are always bickering about who does the most work and who is more important to the operation of the ship. In reality everybody contributes equally, but the jokes still fly. Michigan has two peninsulas and the upper one is commonly abbreviated "U.P." People that live there are called "yoopers." The yoopers call everybody that lives in lower Michigan "trolls" because we live south of the Mackinac Bridge, and trolls live under bridges. Rogers City, Michigan has a huge stone quarry and for years had a large fleet of ships that sailed out of there. Boat crews call Rogers City "Bedrock" and sailors that are from there "Flintstones" or simply "stones." Guys from the next quarry town down the road, Alpena, are "rocks." These are not mean-spirited names but are used in good-natured fun.

I have been so many places on ships it is hard to choose a favorite. Of course, Hawaii is at the top of my list. I have been there three times over the years on ships, and loved it. I was there 12 months ago on a research vessel named the Thomas G. Thompson that was chartered to the University of Washington in Seattle. A friend of mine was the captain and called me up to see if I wanted to come out for a 60-day relief job. It's not every day someone wants to give you a plane ticket to Hawaii so I jumped at the chance.

I also really liked transiting the Panama Canal on the Coast Guard cutter *Woodrush*. It was very tropical and exotic. On the Great Lakes, I like Duluth, Minnesota. The city is built on a hillside and look s like San Francisco at night. It is a busy port and the people (especially the girls!) like sailors and are very friendly.

I've never fallen off a boat but have fallen off the dock before. I was going aboard a ship after vacation and instead of using the regular ramp or "gangway," I tried to come aboard on a plank the deck crew had rigged to work on. Just when I stepped on it, the ship moved away from the dock and the plank, me, and an armload of my stuff all fell in the harbor. I had to swim around in some nasty looking water collecting my gear while all my friends had a good laugh at my expense.

This is getting pretty long so I better stop for now.

Until next time, Smooth Sailing…Lonnie

To aid our circling helicopters in the search for the missing passengers, the Coast Guard crew worked fast to identify all empty *Prinsendam* lifeboats by breaking jars of blue paint in them.

Good Evening Shipmates,

I was happy to get your letter and to hear you enjoyed the pictures I sent! The ones of the ship running in ice are my favorites, too. We were unloading in Saginaw all day and although it was cold and windy it wasn't raining, so I was thankful for that! We are continuing to experience more and more winter-like weather as we get into December. No ice on the lakes yet but it can be seen around the edges of harbors we enter so it won't be long.

Sometimes now, if spray starts flying over the bow, we have to slow down as it freezes fast on deck and we can end up with a foot of rock hard ice covering the hatches and winches up forward. Then the crew has to spend hours with hot water hoses trying to melt enough off to open the hatches. It can take over 48 hours of nonstop work if it gets too thick!

From your questions, I can tell you like my sea stories, so here's another one. It was a dark and stormy night, and I had the watch on the quarterdeck of the Coast Guard cutter *Woodrush*, moored at our dock in Sitka, Alaska. My job in port was to answer the ship's phones and radios, and check the crew on and off the ship. Suddenly the "hot-line" phone, connecting us to the search and rescue dispatcher in Juneau, rang. It seemed that a big Holland-America Co. cruise ship called the *Prinsendam* was on fire 240 miles out in the Gulf of

Alaska, due west of Sitka.

Now this was October, late in the year and nasty offshore. The ship was carrying 586 passengers and crew and most of the passengers were elderly. By the time we got the call, they were abandoning ship and taking to the lifeboats. Our best speed was 10 mph so we would take almost 24 hours to arrive on scene. We recalled everybody we could find, but blew out of town leaving half the crew behind!

Also heading out at top speed from other ports were Coast Guard helicopters and a large high-seas patrol cutter that happened to be in the area. Flying in high wind and blackout conditions, the helicopters were first on the scene. By now the lifeboats were scattered all over and the choppers didn't have a lot of fuel left.

Luckily a supertanker with a load of crude oil out of Valdez, Alaska was in the vicinity. The tanker was called the *Williamsburg*, and had a helicopter landing pad on her deck. The choppers started lifting people out of the lifeboats and ferrying them to the tanker. When they ran out of fuel, they set down on the deck for a ride back to town.

The storm was due to get much worse but one lifeboat full of people was still lost. By now we were on scene and it was really something. The smoke from the burning ship was so thick we could hardly see. When we did see it, she was listed over badly due to all the firefighting water in side. One lifeboat jammed in the boat falls hung crazily off the side and swung slowly against the ship side with a dull booming sound. You could see flames in the wheelhouse windows and hear explosions.

We started searching for the missing lifeboat and knew it was a race against time. All through the night we ran in what is called an "expanding square" search pattern. Near dawn a lookout thought he saw a faint light off in the distance. On the radar just for a moment, was a small blip. We called the faster ship and gave them the coordinates. Sure enough, it was the last lifeboat! Everyone was safe!

As we headed back to town, we were very tired but everybody felt great. The storm turned fierce and we got thrashed but no one cared. It turned out to be the greatest sea rescue in Coast Guard history and we were thrilled to have been a part of it.

The day before Thanksgiving we were loading at Calcite, in Rogers City, Michigan That is pretty close to my house so I called my brother, Tim, and he came over to see me and take a tour of the ship. We went out for lunch and he brought me a bunch of mail so I had a fun day. Tim has his own photography business and is very successful at it. He is a year and a half younger than me and is easily my best friend. We like to canoe the many beautiful rivers in Northern

Michigan and do it 12 months a year, sometimes even when the rivers are frozen in spots!

When Tim graduated from high school, he and a buddy of his flew to Georgia and hiked all the way to Maine on the Appalachian Trail, something like 2400 miles. It took just about 6 months and he was in pretty good shape when they got done!

I had a nice phone chat with Jessica on Thanksgiving. She said to say "Hi" to you all. She wants to be a doctor so studies very hard. Her major in school is in bio-chemistry and she is also studying biology. She only has 20 more days until the end of fall term at school. She will spend Christmas vacation at grandma's while working at a local ski resort. She gave me her Christmas list and I was trying to figure out sizes and colors and, being a guy, getting it all wrong. She was explaining cuffs versus cuffless, inseams, fabrics and all kinds of stuff not in my everyday vocabulary. Finally I just gave her my credit card and told her, "Merry Christmas, Honey, let me know what I got you!" That's what she probably had in mind all the time!

I'll close for now and get this in the mailbag. I have lots more stories to tell you so will write again soon.

Until next time, Fair Winds…Lonnie

Driving a tug in Alaska, hauling bargeloads of glacier silt to be used in building a community baseball diamond.

Good Evening Shipmates,

A stormy week on Lake Superior! After beach-combing our way around the North shore we got to Silver Bay early this morning at "oh-dark-thirty." Weather started getting worse instead of better and we found ourselves in 45 mph northeast winds and 10 to 12-foot seas. The captain came up and decided it was too bad to make the dock, so we just jogged all night. (Jogging means to idle along slowly heading into the wind until it improves.) We were really taking some heavy rolls, and that went on for hours. Finally we turned and ran for cover in Thunder Bay, Ontario, north of Isle Royale. We are anchored now behind Pie Island.

Since we are "riding the hook" tonight, I have a little time to tell some sea stories. They say all true sea stories begin one of two ways: "It was a dark and stormy night" or "Now this is no lie..." Most sailors are great tellers of tales and I have heard both many times.

So I'll tell you about some of the more interesting accidents I saw on the Alaska ferry boats. Especially on the M/V *Tustumena*. That was the only ship in the fleet that ran a totally ocean route so the weather was always bad. The crew had to chain down every vehicle that came aboard, with each car getting four chains to hold it in place. Big construction equipment and tractor-trailers were jacked into position and chained down with heavy-duty chains and binders. We had to check the lashings constantly in high seas to make sure nothing broke loose, but every now and then something would let go and we would have a real surprise on the car deck.

Now this is no lie, once a load of drill pipe snapped its chains during a storm and just flattened a camper pick-up truck parked next to it. You should have seen the owner's face when he came down to drive off the ship! Another time a big semi-trailer broke its chains on a particularly heavy roll and slammed down on its side, crushing a little yellow sports car. The next roll stood it back the other way so when the owner came down, he found his car flat as a pancake, with the impression of it in the side of the semi-trailer!

Another time, it was a dark and stormy night on the run out to Kodiak Island, and we had a herd of very expensive cattle on board for a ranch. We were really taking a beating and the ship was rocking and rolling. I was on duty on the bridge when we got a call that there was an emergency on the car deck. I got down there and found the rancher helping one of his prize cows deliver a calf. We helped him and he was so happy he named the new baby "Tusty," which was the ship's nickname.

I'll keep this short tonight as I know you are busy this week. Your teacher told me you were helping with the Christmas program and having a party. What fun! Have a great time and be safe.

Fair winds…Lonnie

The officer's dining room on the *Buffalo*.

Good Evening Shipmates,

We were getting waxed by the wind today, so we are anchored again, this time in Lake Erie. One gale after another has been ripping through the Lake and we are on day 10 of this load. The crew calls it "the trip with no end." We tried to get into Cleveland this afternoon but with 10-foot seas and 45-50 mph winds out of the west, it was no go. I'm on middle-of-the-night watch so will answer a few of your questions.

Before I started sailing, I did a lot of different things, but they were just jobs, not a career. In high school I went to Wisconsin every summer where my grandparents and uncle had dairy farms. I worked for them doing all sorts of fun stuff. I really liked driving the tractors as you didn't need to be 16 or have a driver's license to drive them on the roads.

Roy is reading over my shoulder and says "Hi." He says it takes 3 minutes and 30 seconds to do a lap of the deck. Crew members walk the deck for exercise and he said he was bored once and timed them while looking out the pilothouse window. Now the decks are so icy that nobody goes out unless they have to. Sometimes guys have to fasten special sandals to their shoes with spikes on the bottom so they can get forward.

We have a new cook on board named Kelly. I knew her from another ship and was glad to see her. She is a very good cook so our lives have improved. She always does extra things to make our meals nicer. She is printing up a fancy menu for Christmas dinner and I will send you one.

The crew is getting pretty goofy as we get toward the end. Somebody is always either singing or quacking like a duck on the radio when we are loading. I think I know who it is but can't be sure. We all are looking forward to lay-up.

The stone docks won't be operating much longer. We should wrap up our year probably around the first week in January. I'll be sorry I won't be able to spend Christmas with Jessica, but she will be with her grandma and cousins and will have a good time. She knows when I come home it will be Christmas all over again. I talked to her the other day and she was studying hard for final exams. She wants to visit her mom in Oregon for spring break so for a surprise I already bought her a plane ticket!

You wanted to know about Christmas on the *Buffalo*. We have a big dinner, much like Thanksgiving, but as a watch stander we still work our 8 hours. I try not to think about it being Christmas, because it doesn't feel like it, and it is easy to be sad and lonely on days like that. It's part of the job though and I'm not one to dwell on negative aspects.

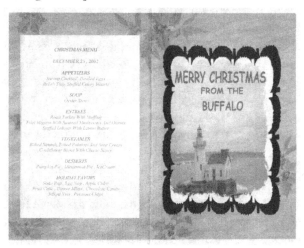

Christmas dinner was always a special meal.

Over the years I have had some fun times on ships at Christmas. Once, in the Coast Guard, I set up a deal with the crew and the captain where all the single guys would take duty over Christmas so the married guys could be home.

In return, the married guys took our duty the weekend before. Us single guys rented a cabin out in the woods in Alaska and a Coast Guard helicopter flew us all out for three days. The ship provided all our food and equipment and even sent holiday decorations. We had a blast!

Another good Christmas memory I have was in 1986 on the Alaska State ferry *Tustumena*. We were on a run between Seward and Kodiak and I was on the midnight watch. It was a clear cold night on the Gulf of Alaska and we were running easy on a big ocean swell. The stars were so big and bright it looked like you could touch them.

The mate said, "Wow, look at that," and we all ran out on the deck to see. It was the Northern Lights, just blazing away in the sky. Big sheets of color, green, blue and red, shaking and shimmering in a curtain of light. It was so beautiful, I was awestruck.

We called the passengers to come see and soon there were 50 people on the roof of the ship. Someone started singing Christmas songs and we all joined in. We must have stayed out watching for two hours. It was really something to remember!

Here on the Lakes, the ships used to go all out to see who could string more lights and displays on the boats. It would be quite a sight as a line of ships moved through the rivers all decorated up. These days, that is no longer done as all the various company lawyers decided that if a ship had an accident, the Christmas lights might be confused with the navigational running lights. So no more Christmas lights on the Great Lakes! : (

No, we don't have a gift shop on board. The *Buffalo*, while a big nice ship, is a working vessel and is pretty basic. The passenger vessels I worked on all had very nice convenience stores, but we are a far cry from that here. Also, no fireplace. The laws regarding ships are very firm about fire prevention so the thought of a fireplace would be enough to turn an inspector green.

Since I was born in Alaska and lived there so long, my favorite holiday is October 18, Alaska Day. It is a big thing in Alaska as it marks the anniversary of the transfer of ownership of the territory of Alaska from Russia to the United States. This was done on October 18, 1867, in Sitka. At the time of the transfer, Sitka was the Russian capital of Alaska and called New Archangel.

Today the day is marked throughout the state as a legal holiday, but it is a weeklong celebration in Sitka. There are parades, dinners, formal balls and all kinds of activities. When Jessica's mother and I were married, we picked that day because it was already special and there was lots going on for our out-of-town guests to see and do.

Bob is back and says "Hi." We had a bunch of guys get off so I got promoted to second mate and had to move to the afternoon and midnight watch, so I'm not on Bob's watch. We still visit at the watch changes though and he reads all your letters.

Well, I've rambled on long enough for tonight. Time to do some of the never-ending paperwork that all ships run on.

Until next time, Smooth Sailing…Lonnie

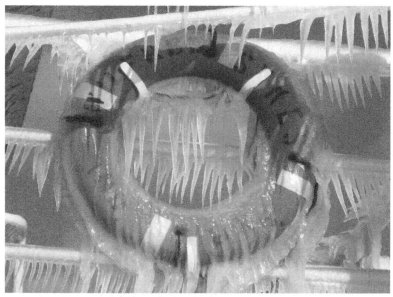

A chilly day on the Great Lakes.

Good Afternoon Shipmates,

It's the day after Christmas and we are downbound in Lake Huron with a load of flux stone (a kind of limestone used in the steel-making process). Yesterday, we caught a major break and arrived at the dock in Stoneport at 10:00 on Christmas day. The dock was closed until 19:00 that night so we got to sit there all day. Lots of the crew (both "rocks" and "stones") live nearby and were able to go home and spend the day with their families. I called Jessica and she and my mom drove over to visit me. They brought mail and presents and we had a great time.

Kelly and the other cooks really went all out and put on a fantastic dinner. They left the galley open all afternoon so we could snack on left overs, just like at home. Another ship called the S.S. *Kaye Barker* was also due at the dock the same day. When two ships are racing for a dock, we go into what we call the "stealth mode," trying not to talk on the radio or give our position away. Lots of her crew were from the Stoneport area too, so we knew if we didn't beat them in, we would be the ones anchored out in the harbor gazing wistfully at the beach!

Coming up the Lake, we had to stop at the fuel dock and needed 70,000 gallons to fill up, and a bunch of lube oil. That would take almost three hours. Since we didn't know where the *Barker* was, the captain shut the fueling down after only 30,000 gallons (instead of filling up, that's called "taking a sip"). It's a good thing he did, as we no sooner got to the loading dock when here came the *Barker*, no more than an hour behind us!

We will be going back to Stoneport this next trip for a cargo of stone, then up to Silver Bay, Minnesota for a load of taconite bound for Cleveland. One more Silver Bay after that and we should be done for the year, around January 7. That all depends on the weather of course, but it has been a little warmer than normal and the ice is nowhere near as bad as usual.

I'll sign off for now. Smooth Sailing…Lonnie

My buddy, Ricardo, getting some sun on Steel Beach, using ear protectors for sunglasses. (You can tell we are in Alaska by how pale he is.)

Good Afternoon Shipmates,

Happy New Year! We are at the dock in Marquette, Mi trying to get this cargo of stone out of the boat. We have a load of some very fine sandy limestone that is known for difficult unloads. It packs into the holds tightly and doesn't want to run onto the belts. The crew has to go into the tunnel and beat on the bottom of the hold with sledge hammers to get the stuff moving. It is a very labor intensive and time-consuming process.

A normal unload of this much tonnage should take around five hours. We have been at this for *48 hours* with at least another twelve to go. Another American Steamship Co. boat was in at the ore dock across town and sent some of her crew over to help. The company also called guys in off vacation from as far away as 200 miles to help.

The only good thing about this deal is that with the delay, we lost the second Silver Bay trip and will probably go up and load for Cleveland, unload and go to the lay-up dock! We are all ready for that. I am looking forward to a couple months off. I have a trip planned at the end of January to go to Key West, Florida. I have a Mustang convertible reserved for three weeks. Considering the temperature here is 9 degrees F and the windchill factor is somewhere near 40 below zero, all I'm thinking about are palm trees and white sandy beaches!

Anyway, the first thing we need to do is get this stone off the ship so I better close. Smooth Sailing…Lonnie

Good Morning Shipmates,

Just came on watch, downbound in Lake Superior. We finally got our load of stone out of the boat at Marquette and loaded iron ore pellets in Silver Bay last night. We thought we were on our last run, but as usually happens, the office may start "one-tripping" us. That happens at the end of the year when each trip our dispatcher says, "just one more."

It drives us all nuts as we have all put in a long season and are thinking about being home. We know how it goes though, and is just part of the job. After a long stretch on board, lay-up is like Christmas, your birthday and the Fourth of July all rolled into one! No matter what, it won't be long now.

We are starting to get into traffic as we get close to Whitefish Point as that is another "choke point." Better get back to work.

Until next time, Fair Winds…Lonnie

A Coast Guard bos'n mate—secured to the cutter with a
safety belt—makes an inspection round in heavy seas.

Good Evening Shipmates,

I'm on a stormy midnight watch. We got "one-tripped" like we thought, so instead of going to the lay-up dock, we find ourselves upbound in Lake Huron bound for Silver Bay again. Some of the guys are crying and moaning like little babies about the extra trip, but I don't really mind it myself. I like sailing this time of year and can always use another week's pay. Partly because of the military build-up in the Middle East, the steel mills want to stockpile as much raw material as possible before the boats stop running. It's interesting how world events trickle down to even affect our work here on the Lakes.

On the bow of a tug on the Lakes, a hand-knit hat from Aunt Lois worked great for staying warm.

It is very cold tonight, with actual temperatures around 5-10 degrees F. With a 40 mph wind blowing out of the west, the wind chill is off the chart. Working on deck requires a full set of heavy winter gear, with felt-lined boots, face masks, and even goggles to protect our eyes. If it wasn't for the individual decals and pictures on our hard-hats it would be difficult to recognize each other! Sitting on a tropical beach is sounding better and better!

We are rolling pretty good but expect the weather to worsen. We have to cross Saginaw Bay and that is a big chunk of open water with western exposure so in a west wind, the seas really build up there. Sometimes we can't get across and have to turn around and "jog" until the wind drops.

This will definitely be our last trip for the year. We should be back down to Cleveland next Monday, the 13th, and at the lay-up dock in Toledo on the 14th.

It takes a couple days to get the boat ready for winter and the deck crew leaves. The engine-room crew stays on for another 2 weeks as there is a lot to do to winterize the engines.

Time to go back to work so will close for now. Until next time, Smooth Sailing…Lonnie

A winter day on the S.S. *Arthur M. Anderson*,
the last ship to see the *Edmund Fitzgerald*.

Good Evening Shipmates,

I just came on watch and was glad to get your letter. We are at anchor up in Lake Superior, hiding from a bad storm. Our present situation is an interesting one. Last trip up to Superior was a nice cruise, little wind, sunshine and a flat calm sea. We knew it couldn't last and when they one-tripped us back up here, I was sure we would have to pay. Well, pay we did, in a big way, and we're still paying!

We fought ice all the way up the St. Marys River to the Soo Locks at Sault Ste. Marie (pronounced "Soo-Saint-Marie", or just called "the Soo"). The weather report wasn't good but we left anyway hoping to get across the lake before the storm hit. We didn't make it. Three hours west of Whitefish Point we drove right into a full-blown West Gale. Winds over 50 mph and huge seas. Nowhere to hide and too dangerous to turn around.

We slowed down so the boat wouldn't pound so hard and just eased on down our track. It is exciting to be in the pilothouse at night in a storm. There is lots to do as we really monitor the gauges closely and are constantly fixing our position on the chart. We have the searchlight on a lot to see when the next set of waves will hit us and we sometimes slow down even more if they look big. The ship is bouncing and flexing and shaking like a wet dog when we take a hard hit. It goes something like BIG ROLL RIGHT…BIG ROLL LEFT… BOW GOES WAY UP AND BOOM…SHAKE SHAKE SHAKE, it buries itself in the next wave and the sequence starts all over again.

The wind was blowing so hard we had to steer 40 degrees to the right of our course to keep moving down our desired track, so we crabbed our way across the lake. When we got to Silver Bay, it was too bad to get in so we ran almost to Duluth before we could get turned around and head back. We finally got in and loaded, and had just left when the next storm front hit us. We kept going for 9 hours until we got here to Thunder Bay.

There are 4 other ships here besides us, three of us from American Steamship Co and two from our partner company Oglebay-Norten. We are all on the "ore train," hauling to Cleveland, and all got one-tripped. The Soo Locks close for the year in 5 days, on the 15th, so everybody is sweating making the deadline and not getting stuck on Lake Superior until spring.

The weather report is still bad but eventually we will have to make a move. We will probably start beachcombing around the lake, going from one protected bay to another, until we can make a run for it. The crew is going wild as we are supposed to be at the lay-up dock instead of getting our butts kicked around Lake Superior.

Roy just told me that he is bored (nothing to do on anchor watch but look out the window) and that I was being poor company tonight, so I better wrap this up.

Until next time, Fair Winds…Lonnie

Good Evening Shipmates,

The adventure continues. After I wrote last, we stayed in Thunder Bay a while longer, then decided to make a run for Whitefish Point and the Soo Locks. The weather report was still bad and boats that left before us were taking a beating. We would have stayed longer but one of our crewmen is diabetic and had run out of insulin. His blood sugar was climbing and the nearest medicine was waiting at the marine post office at the Soo. The captain had to decide if he should call the Coast Guard to send a helicopter for him or try to make it across the lake.

We took off around 18:00 and by the time Roy and I came on watch, we were our past Isle Royale in open water. This time, instead of beating into big waves, the wind was coming at us from the side, so we were rolling badly. BIG-TIME.

Normally we would adjust our course to put the wind and sea on our quarter (off the bow or off the stern) but we couldn't go right because it was worse that way. And we couldn't go left because there was a shoal (rocks) that way. We just had to take it all night long. At one point I went down to get something from my room, and my bed and desk had torn loose from their hooks and were smashing around. All over the ship things were breaking and flying around. I finally edged closer than I liked to the rocks just so we could get a better ride.

When we do that, I take fixes and put them on the chart every 10 minutes to make sure I know exactly where we are. All this sounds kind of scary, but after you have done it for as long as I have, it's more of a pain than anything. I always tease Roy when we are getting thrashed, saying, "Come on, Roy, admit it…you love this!" I can't repeat some of the things he says back to me!

The 1000-footer *American Spirit* stuck in the ice while a Coast Guard icebreaker circles the boat to cut us free.

Finally, we made it to the Soo Locks and Greg got his medicine. We thought we were home free but there is another fierce gale on Lake Huron. Also, as we got down the river toward DeTour, Michigan, the ice started getting thick (almost a foot thick). We couldn't get out on the lake tonight so instead of anchoring we just pushed into the ice and stopped.

Right now the ice is all around us and if I dared, I could probably climb off the ship and walk to shore. This last trip is really turning into a marathon.

I usually don't care how long these trips take, but thought I would be home by the 16th so made plans with Jessica to spend the weekend at home. Now it looks like I may not be home before next week, so that bothers me. We will get there when we get there, however, and it doesn't pay to get in a hurry. We all know that, but it's been a long season and we are ready to be done.

We still have to go all the way to Cleveland, and unload at two docks there before we can go to Toledo and lay-up the boat. The bright side is that the pay is very good this time of year, so I'm not crying too much!

Time to go take some weather observations. Until next time, Smooth Sailing…Lonnie

Downbound in the Detroit River in January, aboard *American Republic,* following an icebreaker's track.

Good Afternoon Shipmates,

Great news! Finally we arrived at the lay-up dock in Toledo at noon today. Tough trip right till the last minute. Howling blizzards and ice so thick that at times we were only going 1.2 mph at full engine speed. Everyone is very busy now with final duties getting ready to leave tomorrow. I only have a minute but wanted to let you know we finished our season safely.

Until next time, Smooth Sailing…Lonnie

Sailing into the sunset, with calm seas and
eager anticipation of whatever tomorrow may bring.

3 and 2
(long long long short short)

About the Author

Lon Calloway grew up in Upper Michigan, an ambitious oldest child with aspirations of living an exciting life. By the time he finished high school, he had lived in Norway as a foreign-exchange student, and touched down in Sweden, Denmark, Ireland, Hawaii, American Samoa, Tahiti and New Zealand. Lon had big plans.

After three years of studies at Michigan State to become a teacher, he applied to the Maritime academy in Traverse City, Michigan. After all, he'd been drawing pictures of boats since he was a small boy. But upon learning he would have to start over from scratch, he decided on another plan. Lon joined the Coast Guard.

There he was guaranteed to receive navigation training—for free, no less—plus he would get paid. *And* they promised duty in Alaska. Win-win-win. Only later would he discover Alaska was considered a Coast Guard penal colony, and that a posting there wasn't difficult to get. In the end, the price Lon paid was higher than expected, but he did get all the training he was after. All in all, he was pleased with the arrangement.

Lon Calloway on a boat somewhere in Alaska:
"I can't believe I'm getting paid for this."

After completing his service in the Coast Guard, Lon spent a couple years on Great Lakes iron ore freighters. He was working eight hours on and then 16 hours off, with nothing to do but watch the water roll past. This, he knew, was not the life he'd envisioned for himself.

After a few semi-permanent positions, Lon became wary of taking a permanent job with a company where a dispatcher would dictate when he could get off the boat. Instead he opted to carve a career out of being a relief. He would fly in like Superman to save some poor soul's day, who couldn't go home until their relief showed up. Who doesn't want to be *that* hero? If they liked him and he liked them, he could extend his stay another 30 days, allowing another guy to go on vacation.

Over the years, Lon had affiliations with five maritime unions, plus he had an agent. Typically, within 24 hours of making a call, he could be back on boat and geared up for his next adventure. The connections Lon made this way served him very well, allowing him to forego the more traditional path of many other shipmates, that often involved working in an office or becoming a dispatcher themselves.

In 40-plus years, Lon did relief work on over 85 boats and ships including a 40-foot wooden halibut long-liner in Alaska, a Steel shrimp dragger in Key West, a research ship in Hawaii, a Coast Guard cutter in the Gulf of Alaska, a ferry boat to Mackinac Island and various ferries on the Alaska Marine Highway System, plus a 1000-foot monster of an iron ore freighter on the Great Lakes. Lon began his career as a dishwasher and ended it holding Unlimited Captain/First Class Pilot papers for Great Lakes inland waters, as well as Master of Towing papers for work on tugboats in coastal waters.

All in all, Captain Lon has had the time of his life, enjoying every colorful adventure as well as the hard work that went with them. Lon is now retired and living in Indian River, Michigan where he and Lisa offer history tours on their charming wooden boat. His Monkey Fist zipper pulls are a customer favorite.

A miniature example of the baseball-size
Monkey Fist still in use on ships today.

Captain Lon sailing along with Captain Nemo
on his Crooked River history boat tour.

Publisher's Note

I am so grateful for the experience of collaborating with my cousin Lon to publish his sea stories. I first became aware of them when I found them in a binder at my parents' cabin in Northern Wisconsin. My dad, whose sister is Lon's mom, was especially enamored with them and highly encouraged all of us to read them. "They are just so good," he said.

One of the things I love about this is that my parents are in their eighties and both lifelong devout Lutherans. And yet there is so much heart in these fascinating stories—along with a ton of humor and touch of salt—that it makes our own hearts sing when we read them. At least mine did.

In my book, this is the essence of what it means to be spiritual: to uncover our inner light and let it shine out into the world. *Nicely done, Cuz.*

– Jill Loree
Founder of Phoenesse